*Native American Music in
Eastern North America*

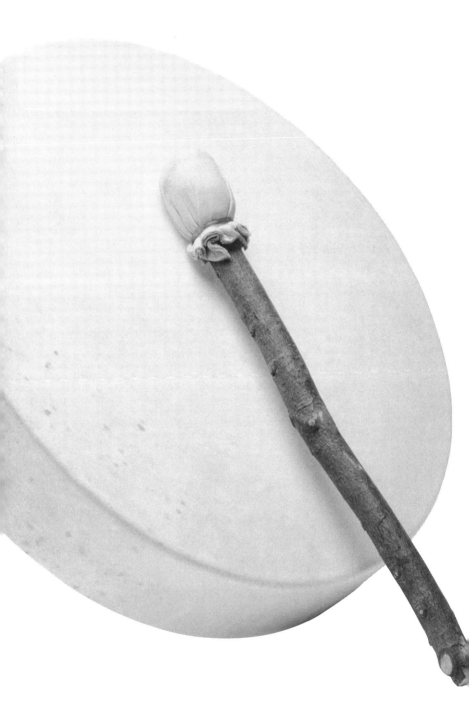

Native American Music in Eastern North America

〜

EXPERIENCING MUSIC, EXPRESSING CULTURE

∞

BEVERLEY DIAMOND

New York   Oxford
OXFORD UNIVERSITY PRESS
2008

Oxford University Press, Inc., publishes works that further Oxford University's
objective of excellence in research, scholarship, and education.

Oxford   New York
Auckland   Cape Town   Dar es Salaam   Hong Kong   Karachi
Kuala Lumpur   Madrid   Melbourne   Mexico City   Nairobi
New Delhi   Shanghai   Taipei   Toronto

With offices in
Argentina   Austria   Brazil   Chile   Czech Republic   France   Greece
Guatemala   Hungary   Italy   Japan   Poland   Portugal   Singapore
South Korea   Switzerland   Thailand   Turkey   Ukraine   Vietnam

Published by Oxford University Press, Inc.
198 Madison Avenue, New York, New York 10016
http://www.oup.com

Oxford is a registered trademark of Oxford University Press

Library of Congress Cataloging-in-Publication Data
Diamond, Beverley, 1948-
    Native American music in eastern North America : experiencing music,
expressing culture / Beverley Diamond.
        p. cm. — (Global music series)
    Includes bibliographical references and index.
    ISBN-13: 978-0-19-530104-5 (paper (main))
    ISBN-13: 978-0-19-530103-8 (cloth)
    1. Indians of North America—Music—History and criticism. 2. Indians of
North America—Music—Social aspects. 3. Indians of North America—Social life
and customs.   I. Title.

ML3550.D53 2008
781.62'97074—dc22   2007014405

Printing number: 9 8 7 6 5 4 3 2 1

Printed in the United States of America
on acid-free paper

GLOBAL MUSIC SERIES

General Editors: Bonnie C. Wade and Patricia Shehan Campbell

Music in East Africa, Gregory Barz
Music in Central Java, Benjamin Brinner
Teaching Music Globally, Patricia Shehan Campbell
Native American Music in Eastern North America, Beverley Diamond
Carnival Music in Trinidad, Shannon Dudley
Music in Bali, Lisa Gold
Music in Ireland, Dorothea E. Hast and Stanley Scott
Music in China, Frederick Lau
Music in Egypt, Scott L. Marcus
Music in Brazil, John P. Murphy
Music in America, Adelaida Reyes
Music in Bulgaria, Timothy Rice
Music in North India, George E. Ruckert
Mariachi Music in America, Daniel Sheehy
Music in West Africa, Ruth M. Stone
Music in the Andes, Thomas Turino
Music in South India, T. Viswanathan and Matthew Harp Allen
Music in Japan, Bonnie C. Wade
Thinking Musically, Bonnie C. Wade

Contents

Foreword

∞

In the past three decades interest in music around the world has surged, as evidenced in the proliferation of courses at the college level, the burgeoning "world music" market in the recording business, and the extent to which musical performance is evoked as a lure in the international tourist industry. This heightened interest has encouraged an explosion in ethnomusicological research and publication, including production of reference works and textbooks. The original model for the "world music" course—if this is Tuesday, this must be Japan—has grown old, as has the format of textbooks for it, either a series of articles in single multiauthored volumes that subscribe to the idea of "a survey" and have created a canon of cultures for study, or single-authored studies purporting to cover world musics or ethnomusicology. The time has come for a change.

This Global Music Series offers a new paradigm. Instructors can now design their own courses; choosing from a set of case study volumes, they can decide which and how much music they will teach. The series also does something else; rather than uniformly taking a large region and giving superficial examples from several different countries within it, case studies offer two formats—some focused on a specific culture, some on a discrete geographical area. In either case, each volume offers greater depth than the usual survey. Themes significant in each instance guide the choice of music that is discussed. The contemporary musical situation is the point of departure in all the volumes, with historical information and traditions covered as they elucidate the present. In addition, a set of unifying topics such as gender, globalization, and authenticity occur throughout the series. These are addressed in the framing volume, *Thinking Musically* (Wade), which sets the stage for the case studies by introducing those topics and other ways to think about how people make music meaningful and useful in their lives. *Thinking Musically* also presents the basic elements of music as they are practiced in musical systems around the world so that authors of each case study do not have to spend time explaining them and can delve immediately into the particular music. A second framing volume, *Teaching Music*

Globally (Campbell), guides teachers in the use of *Thinking Musically* and the case studies.

The series subtitle, "Experiencing Music, Expressing Culture," also puts in the forefront the people who make music or in some other way experience it and also through it express shared culture. This resonance with global studies in such disciplines as history and anthropology, with their focus on processes and themes that permit cross-study, occasions the title of this Global Music Series.

Bonnie C. Wade
Patricia Shehan Campbell
General Editors

Preface

∽

Until I decided to accept the invitation to write this book, I had always vowed that I would never write a textbook. I am more interested in exploring the uses and limitations of authority than setting down what students inevitably would regard as an authoritative version, a truth about the musical practices of a group of people. As it turns out, by working with a group of Aboriginal advisors whose knowledge was so deep and whose capacity to discuss issues of representation was so capable, I found the preparation of this book one of the most rewarding projects I have ever undertaken. I hope that the differences among our perspectives remain clear and that this textbook, then, can never be read simply as a univocal authoritative text.

Writing about Native American music cultures involved a number of specific challenges. There is not, and has never been, an adequate textbook about "Native American Music," and as one reviewer of the manuscript said, there probably never can be. Even though people may speak about Native American culture in the singular, it is clear that the cultures of the more than five hundred nations are distinctive and unique, not reducible to a single account. This Global Music Series has taken a middle ground approach to the challenge of including a diverse array of Native American histories and cultures. The editors have commissioned books by region—still challenging assignments but justifiable in that certain historic commonalities and layers of interaction both among diverse native communities and between First Nations / Inuit and Euro- or African Americans can be acknowledged. This volume deals with the northern and eastern parts of North America. The Northeast is covered in more detail than the Southeast quite simply because my experience (and that of my advisors) is located there.

A second challenge is the clear need for indigenous perspectives and yet the relative sparsity (though growing number) of ethnomusicologists of First Nations, Métis, or Inuit descent. I struggled with the decision to speak as an outsider about cultures that are able to speak so eloquently on their own behalf. In addition to indigenous perspectives, however, I firmly believe that we need dialogue: dialogue that does not gloss over the shared responsibilities that we have toward social justice, the environment, and peaceful coexistence. Many share an interest in how music by Native Americans is used in relation to these common issues. To create a text that compared perspectives, then, became a clear objective.

A third challenge in writing about Native American culture is the mismatching of languages for concepts that, in English, we call "music," "song," etc. Even more problematic is the inevitable reductionism in musical transcriptions. The subtleties of timbre or pulse relationships, for instance, are not easily reflected in Western notation systems. Both the English language, then, and the look of music transcriptions are prone to oversimplify. Some of the suggested activities in the book encourage students and teachers to think about and discuss such issues of representation.

A fourth challenge are the stereotypes, particularly the colonial propensity of many previous publications to render Native American culture ahistorical, in a sort of timeless past. Native American modernity remains underrepresented. In addition, the need for further research on the histories of song genres and specific repertoire remains. What we have tried to do here, however, is to demonstrate how musical practices have often developed in response to social circumstances, to colonialism in particular.

In light of these challenges, the identification of themes for this book was not difficult. The need for indigenous perspectives is addressed by examining both the definition and the problematic reductionism of what is now called "traditional indigenous knowledge." It is further addressed by the inclusion of perspectives from the three Aboriginal project advisors. The need for careful history that accounts for the relationships among North American communities at different periods of time and in different circumstances is addressed by the theme of "encounter." The need for representations of Native American modernity and for a better understanding of the ways that past traditions inform contemporary indigenous life is addressed by focusing on contemporary musical practices, particularly in Chapter 5. Running through all of these themes is a commitment to demonstrate divergent experiences and points of view. It has become clear, for instance, that men and women experienced colonialism somewhat differently. Gender, then, becomes one of the threads that laces through the themes of this book.

Finally, the importance placed on dialogue opens a space for readers. Many of the "Activities" in this text require readers to reflect on their own values, their own strength and weakness of observation, and their own approaches to some of the issues we raise. The classroom affords a very privileged and fruitful space for comparing further reflections, then, and I hope that classroom discussions are always a central part of the pedagogy of teachers who use this book. Of course, most of all, I hope that the beauty, balance, and creativity of the Native Americans you will get to know in this textbook will transform your life as they have transformed mine.

Please note that, in addition to the CD in this book, there is an iMix available at *www.oup.com/us/globalmusic*

ACKNOWLEDGMENTS

I want especially to thank Sadie Buck, Stephen Augustine, and Karin Kettler for collaborating on this project. Their wise advice, important corrections, wonderful stories, and friendship were gifts I appreciate very much. Thanks to Cliff for sharing the pleasure of participating in a number of First Nations powwows, concerts, and other gatherings over the years; for his insightful discussions of so many issues related to this work; and for his support and good humor throughout the process. I want to thank Bonnie Wade for her stimulating comments on my drafts and her superb editorial skill, and Patricia Campbell for her ever-positive responses. Thanks to Maureen Houston, assistant extraordinaire at the MMaP Research Centre (Memorial University of Newfoundland) and the best interview transcriber I have ever known. Thanks to Cory Schneider, who expedited the project as editorial assistant for the Press, to production editor Lisa Grzan, and Teresa Nemeth, whose copy editing helped make the text speak more clearly. I am grateful to the five readers for Oxford University Press, whose suggestions were invaluable in strengthening the final product and whose collegial encouragement was much appreciated: Tara Browner, University of California, Los Angeles; Paula Conlon, University of Oklahoma; Charlotte Frisbie, Southern Illinois University of Edwardsville; Anna Hoefnagels, Carleton University; Victoria Levine, Colorado College; and Gordon E. Smith, Queen's University. As usual, any errors or misrepresentations that remain are my responsibility.

CD Track List

1. "An Arctic Lullaby" ("The Ptarmigan and the Snow Bunting") Narrated by Jeannie Arreak-Kullalik. *Inuit Legends*, vol. 2 [English], CBC North Radio One, 2003.

2. "Life Force." Santee Smith, composer. *Kaha:wi*. SS98609. Self-produced, n.d.

3. "Travelling Song." Aboriginal Women's Voices Group (various artists). *Hearts Of The Nations*. AWV/Banff 97, 1997.

4. "Juggling Game Song." Unidentified singers. Field recording by B. Diamond, 1981.

5. "*Qiarvaaq*." Betty Peryuaq and Hattie Atutuva. *Throat Singing Conference*. Avataq Cultural Institute, 2001.

6. "*Qimmiruluapik*." Lucy Amaroalik and Alacie Tulaugak. *Throat Singing Conference*. Avataq Cultural Institute, 2001.

7. "Seagull/ *Naujaq*." Karin and Kathy Kettler. *Throat Singing Conference*. Avataq Cultural Institute, 2001.

8. "E5-770, My Mother's Name." Lucie Idlout. *E5-770, My Mother's Name*, Heart Wreck Records AR-20432, 2002.

9. "*Shuk tshi naskumitin*." Mani Shan Nui. Field recording by B. Diamond, 1982.

10. "Santu's Song." Santu Toney. Field recording by Frank Speck, 1910.

11. "Mte'skmuey / Mi'kmaq Snake Dance" (Kitpu Singers). *Denny Family: Mi'kmaq Chants*, Kewniq Recordings, Eskasoni, n.d.

12. "*I'ko*." Susan Hill. MMaP studio recording by B. Diamond, 2006.

13. "Mi'kmaq Ko'jua" (Sarah Denny). *Denny Family: Mi'kmaq Chants*, Kewniq Recordings, Eskasoni, n.d.

14. "Pine Cone Dance." Spirit of the Dawn. *Songs of the Wabanaki*, Penobscot Indian Arts, 2001.

15. "Eskanye Set." Gordie Buck. Field recording by Sam Cronk, 1985.

16. "Peter Cottontail (*eskanye*)." Composed by Alfred Keye and Floyd Harris. Old Mush Singers. *Ojihgwaga:yo: Old Mush Singers*, vol. 1, independent production, n.d.

17. "Smoke Dance"—slow and fast (track 12). Kyle Dowdy Sr. Recorded at Grand River powwow, 1999. *Smoke Dance*, Ohwe-jagehka: Ha'degaenage:, n.d.

18. "Rattle Songs (1–3)." Ulali (Pura Fe, Soni Moreno, Jennifer Kreisberg). *Makh Jchi*, Corn Beans and Squash Music, 1997.

19. "The Mystery Stepdancer." Lee Cremo. *The Champion Returns*, Cremo Productions LC9501, n.d.

20. "My Way." Forever. *Something to Dream Of*, Forever Music Group, STDOCD1012, 2004.

21. "Why We Rhyme." Trurez Crew. *It's Begun*. Trurez Productions, n.d.

22. "Sweet Tobacco." Charlie Panigoniak. *True North Concerts: Truly Something*, Canadian Broadcasting Corporation, 2000.

23. "1492 Who Found Who?" Murray Porter. *1492 Who Found Who*. First Nations Music Publishing Y2-10015.

24. "Museum Cases." Ulali. *Mahk Jchi*, Corn Beans and Squash Music, 1997.

25. "A Postcolonial Tale." Joy Harjo and Poetic Justice. *Letter from the End of the Twentieth Century*, Silver Wave Records SD914, 1997.

26. "Bonegame / *Oma bema*." Excerpts from a preproduction CD of the opera, *BONES*. Courtesy of Sadie Buck, n.d.

Music Selections Available on iMix

1. "Ancestors." Tanya Tagaq Gillus (Inuk) with Bjork. From Bjork's album, *Medulla*.

2. "One Drop of Blood." Cherokee National Choir.

3. "Ko-ju Wa-Kena." Eastern Eagle (Mi'kmaq).

4. "Kepmitetmneg" (Honour Song). Eastern Eagle (Mi'kmaq).

5. Eskanye. Six Nations Women Singers (Seneca/Cayuga). From *We Will All Sing*, SOAR Records.

6. Rabbit Dance. Six Nations Women Singers (Seneca/Cayuga). From *We Will All Sing*, SOAR Records.

7. "Unity Stomp." Robbie Robertson with the Six Nations Women Singers. From *Contact from the Underworld of Redboy*.

8. "Messenger." Joanne Shenandoah (Oneida). From *Life Blood*.

9. Junior Grass Dance. Sizzortail. From *Gathering of Nations 2000*. Volume 2. Southern.

10. Girls Fancy Shawl Dance Song. Red Bull. From *Gathering of Nations 2002*. Volume 1. Northern.

11. Intertribal. Otter Tail. From *Gathering of Nations 1998*.

12. Blackstone. Boys traditional. From *Gathering of Nations. 2000*. Volume 1 (Northern)

13. Stoney Park. Ladies Jingle Dress Song. From *Gathering of Nations*. 1999.

14. Assiniboine Jrs. Ladies Traditional. From *Gathering of Nations*. 1993.

15. Various artists. Men's Fancy Dance Song. From *Gathering of Nations*. 1994.

16. "Stand Up." Susan Aglukark. From *Unsung Heroes*.

17. "Akua Tuta." Kashtin. From *Akua Tuta*.

CHAPTER 1

Traditions of Knowledge: Indigenous Knowledge and the Western Music School

There are few people on earth who have been mythologized as much as Native Americans, as much as First Nations, Inuit, and Métis. The idea of "Indians"—the name a European mistake—has been mythologized by writers of history, anthropology, and fiction, by filmmakers, composers, makers of crafts, and others (see Ellingson 2001; Pisani 2005). The Lakota historian Philip Deloria has written eloquently about the way our expectations of Native Americans have shaped the way we perceive American history and society. Indeed, the invented or imagined stereotypes are so prevalent that they influence all of us. Many indigenous people, however, have written histories, scholarly and fictional studies, made art and music, or become community leaders whose words and actions interrupt the stereotypes.

In the twenty-first century, your classroom undoubtedly has people from many different cultures. You may have Native American ancestry; your family may have roots in Africa, Asia, Europe, or elsewhere. (If there are no Native American students in your school or university classes, you should ask your teachers why not. It used to be that non-Aboriginal teachers dismissed such questions by saying that there were no longer indigenous people in a given region. Such answers, however, were not well informed, since there are many indigenous people in every region of North America and every urban center.) You probably exchange stories with your classmates about your lives, your hopes and dreams, and you quickly realize that while your families may have different traditions, languages, beliefs, or values, everybody's life is both traditional and modern in various ways, and exceedingly complicated.

ACTIVITY 1.1 *Interview a classmate or friend, posing the following questions:*

1. *How do you define "traditional" and "contemporary" music?*
2. *What values do you associate with each type of music?*
3. *Where in your life do you listen to or perform music that you define in each way?*
4. *To whom do you feel a sense of relationship by listening to or performing a particular type of music?*

Your expectations and your findings about the views of others may influence how easily you make friends with someone from a different culture, how deeply you learn a particular subject, or how easily you work in a particular social or physical space. The more open you can be to different perspectives on these issues, the more easily you will understand the different perspectives in this text.

This book will explore contrasting expectations about Native American sound and song, focusing on the northern and eastern regions of North America (Figure 1.1).

FIGURE 1.1 *Map of Native American (Inuit and First Nations) people of the North and East.*

Teachers and students who wish to teach or learn about other indigenous cultures may consult the section entitled "Some Key Publications on the Music and Dance of Other First Nations" in the resources listed at the end of this volume.

Three themes thread through each chapter. One theme is "traditional indigenous knowledge," a phrase that is simultaneously hopeful and problematic. I will ask what relevance traditional indigenous knowledge (which is sometimes abbreviated to TIK in contemporary literature; TEK is "traditional ecological knowledge") has for understanding what English speakers call "music" by comparing some assumptions that underlie the study of music in Euro-American music schools.

Such a comparison already introduces the second theme of the book: encounter. The sound and song traditions of Native Americans make the most sense when they are considered as part of an encounter with different natural and social spheres: the sounds of specific localities, for instance, or the sounds of song traditions from neighbors or foreigners. The theme of "encounter" also encourages comparison between different ways of learning music. I hope that this book will help Native American music students understand some of the differences between the ways they learn in different contexts, and non–Native American students understand that there are rich and valuable ways of hearing and making sound in the world that have been developed in First Nations, Inuit, and Métis cultures. But whose encounter with whom? Different indigenous nations with each other or with the diverse environments they occupy? Native American with European or African American or other societies? First Nations or Inuit as hybrid musicians in contemporary multicultural contexts? Each of these meeting points merits careful consideration.

The third theme of the book is indigenous modernity. Concepts of the "modern" have often been formulated from Eurocentric perspectives. Indigenous artists, however, have their own formulations, often reflected in vibrant contemporary cultural expressions of the late twentieth and early twenty-first centuries.

NAMES MATTER!

The words used in the paragraphs above may already be confusing. If you live in the United States you are probably familiar with the term "Native American" or "American Indian" to refer to more than 550 different groups of indigenous people in your country, although not all have been able to maintain their languages. The word "Aboriginal" is not widely used in the United States and has perjorative connotations for some United States citizens.

Three indigenous groups are customarily identified and recognized in the Canadian constitution of 1982 as the "Aboriginal" people of Canada: First Nations, Inuit, and Métis. In many subsequent Canadian publications, their histories and social issues are differentiated. In Canada, approximately one hundred First Nations groups, four Inuit groups, and Métis people maintain approximately fifty different Aboriginal languages. Here as in the United States, language loss is a serious concern.

Official recognition for Aboriginal people in Canada in 1982 was particularly important to the Métis, people of mixed indigenous and (generally) European descent. The matter of recognizing Métis has been further complicated by challenges of identifying Métis, especially in eastern Canada (see, e.g., Bonita Lawrence 2004). Some Métis organizations in Canada recognize only the historic communities of western Canada, where relatively cohesive cultural practices and distinctive languages have been identified. Strong opposition to this exclusionist boundary making has been voiced in Ontario, Quebec, and Atlantic Canada, however.

With reference to First People, the term "nation" is the norm in Canada, where the parity of governments is an important long-term goal, and this language is also used in many parts of the United States. The word "tribe" is generally regarded as derogatory, north of the border, but acceptable in the United States.

The naming of specific groups is, in reality, a complex matter. Some Native American, First Nations, Inuit, or Métis groups are known by multiple names, some older or newer, some invented by outsiders or community members. Out of respect, this book will generally use the names that people have for themselves. Hence, it uses Inuit (singular is Inuk) rather than Eskimo, Innu rather than Montagnais or Naskapi, Wolastoqiyik rather than Maliseet, Haudenosaunee (spelled variously in some regions) rather than Iroquois, Muscogee rather than Creek, and Wendat rather than Huron, to name only a few. In some cases, older names are used alongside new ones, but communities have adopted more precise spelling systems. Peskotomuhkatiyik replaces Passamaquoddy, for instance. In older publications, you will see Micmac, but the current spelling, Mi'kmaq, is more accurate. Note, however, that Mi'kmaq people call themselves L'nu, and furthermore, the word "Mi'kmaq" may in the first place have been a mistaken transcription of the word "*nikmaq*," meaning "our kin."

Place names have often changed, particularly as local names in indigenous languages have been reclaimed to replace colonial names. In 1999, for instance, a new territory was created in northern Canada and called Nunavut, the Inuit word for "our land." Subsequently, Inuit in northern Quebec claimed the right to call their territory Nunavik, northern Labrador became Nunatsiavut, and the western Canadian Arctic adopted Inuvialuit.

ACTIVITY 1.2 *Find a recent map of Canada and try to locate these recently established regions of the north. In order to sort out the naming practices, compile lists of the names and identifications of individuals, groups, and places as you read this book.*

Names themselves are a good way to introduce the themes already mentioned. Embedded in those names is a concept of place and selfhood that is fundamental to the definition of traditional indigenous knowledge. Replacing names in colonial languages with names in indigenous languages is part of the process of asserting a vision of modernity for First Nations, Inuit, and Métis people. The shifts in naming practices are strongly indicative of the encounters that have shaped the histories of each community or culture.

ACTIVITY 1.3 *Choose one state in the United States or one province or territory in Canada. Do research on the Internet to try to find all the indigenous nations in that region. Try to determine their own names for themselves and compare any other names that have been used.*

WRITING THIS BOOK AS AN ENCOUNTER

Since encounter (and hence, relationship) is an important theme for this book, the concept was built into the process of producing it. As primary author, I have had opportunities to work in a number of communities and to interact with many Native American musicians and elders for several decades, but I am non-Native. I see my role as twofold: to share the knowledge that I have but also to enable a dialogue about the representation of indigenous music in the academy. In order to do this, I invited three wise people to become part of an advisory committee for the book. All live and work with multiple traditions of knowledge. They are Haudenosaunee arts and culture specialist and internationally renowned singer Sadie Buck; hereditary chief of the Mi'kmaq nation, museum curator, and author of work on traditional indigenous science Stephen Augustine; and Chairperson of the Inuit Throat Singers Association Karin Kettler.

Sadie Buck (Figure 1.2) has taught in departments of fine arts, anthropology, indigenous studies, environmental studies, and social work. She is pursuing studies in anthropology and sociology. For forty years, she has been the lead singer of the Six Nations Women Singers, based at Oshwegen, Ontario. She is a transnational musician who has sung at the Olympics, the New Orleans Jazz Festival, the opening of the National Museum of the American Indian in Washington, D.C., as well as conferences in Australia and New Zealand. She founded the Aboriginal Women's Voices program for the Banff Centre for the Arts in Alberta, carrying forward an initiative that has had profound effects for Native American women musicians. She remains one of the foremost culture bearers of the Haudenosaunee people, for whom she has been a clan mother, teacher, and community contributor.

FIGURE 1.2   *Haudenosaunee arts and culture specialist Sadie Buck, from Six Nations, Ontario.*   *(Photo by B. Diamond)*

FIGURE 1.3 *Stephen Augustine, Mi'kmaq hereditary chief and museum curator. (Photo by Andrew Wilson. Used by permission.)*

Stephen Augustine (Figure 1.3) has studied anthropology and history, receiving a master's degree in Canadian studies. He now works as a curator at the Canadian Museum of Civilization. At the same time, he speaks at community workshops and ceremonies when needed. He has written about concepts of indigenous science (Augustine 1997).

Karin Kettler (Figure 1.4) has taught school in Inuit communities in Nunavik, and over the past decade she has learned the art of throat singing in a traditional way from elders, Inuit friends, and relatives. Her heritage is that of the village of Kangiqsualujjuaq in Nunavik, Quebec. Even though she has spent most of her life in southern Canada, Karin has maintained a close connection to her culture. Together with her

FIGURE 1.4 *Karin Kettler, Inuit throat singer, teacher, and president of the Throat Singers Association.* *(Photo Courtesy of Karin Kettler. Used by permission.)*

sister Kathy, in the duo Nukariik, she performs for diverse audiences nationally and internationally, sharing Inuit culture through songs and drumming. She currently does health research for an Aboriginal organization in Ottawa, Ontario.

Our dialogue informs the way Native American music in the north and east is represented. As Chippewa sociologist Duane Champagne has written: "An open and free forum for discussion among Indian and non-Indian scholars benefits everyone who seeks to produce accurate, substantial, and significant studies of Indian peoples . . . Indian nations are human groups, part of the broad history of all humanity, and therefore can be compared with other groups in technology, cultural world views, history and adaptation to global markets and expanding state systems, etc." (1998, 181–2). Nevertheless, the need to pay close attention to as many Native American perspectives as possible is imperative. Teachers and students who read this book are urged to consult the Resources list to find other publications that are authored by Native Americans in order to further understand differences in perspective.

There are currently different views about whether indigenous beliefs, songs, and customs should be shared with outsiders—both members of other tribes or nations and non–Native Americans. In a few cases, people feel the pain of being misrepresented by outsiders over and over again, and, as a result of that, some believe that nothing should be shared, that Native American knowledge should be accessible only to the Native American community from whence it came. In my experience, this is not the majority view although it is an understandable one.

Most First Nations, Métis, and Inuit friends stress that knowledge carries with it obligations and responsibilities. Ceremonial knowledge, for instance, would not be shared with someone who was not in a position to fulfill those obligations and responsibilities. Haudenosaunee have an expression that means "you have to be invited": it implies that only when you are thought to be ready and able to use certain knowledge responsibly, will it be shared. It does not imply that knowledge is secret, but rather that those entrusted with knowledge must know how it should be used. For this reason this book focuses on social traditions rather than ceremonial ones, while recognizing that in some contexts these are not strictly separated. Unless you are a member of a Native American community, you are unlikely to be in a position to accept the responsibility that certain types of ceremonial knowledge entail. On the other hand, the responsibility that relates to the knowledge of social traditions—to act respectfully toward the culture bearers and to help celebrate the gifts of Creation, the gifts that sustain life—is hopefully within your reach.

TRADITIONAL WAYS OF KNOWING

Many indigenous teachers emphasize that experience is a way of knowing. Furthermore, they stress that knowledge and ways of knowing are impossible to distinguish. The process of transmission is part of the knowledge itself. Inuit elders who contributed to a traditional knowledge research project conducted in the early twenty-first century by the Nunavut Arctic College, for instance, began their oral historical accounts by stating that they could only tell what they had experienced.

Their words contrast sharply with ethnographies where the expert outsider has often been credited with more authority than local culture bearers. Such statements by elders remind us that knowledge is relational; knowing is dependent on a local context. Generalizations are consequently dangerous. The elders imply that a local belief or tradition should not be assumed to be a belief or tradition of all Inuit people.

In many Native American cultures, knowledge, including song knowledge, may come as a gift, in a dream perhaps, or from a human or spirit source. Gifts imply relationship. Indeed, as Stephen Augustine emphasized to me, the songs and dances reflect the experiential relationships of humans and animals. Without knowledge of the relationship, the gift (of song or dance) is less meaningful. Elders who spend their lives understanding the deep, deep knowledge of a specific place and community, who maintain the stories, ways of remembering precise sounds, motions, and visual details of the environment they live in, have an admirable and valuable profundity of spirit and intellect.

It is important to recognize, however, that local knowledge is neither homogeneous nor isolated. Most modern people—indigenous and nonindigenous—have cross-cultural encounters, travel, or use various media and communication technologies that provide access to diverse social worlds. Powwow organizers, for instance, recognize the importance of the Internet in circulating their protocols and descriptions of the meanings of various dances. Cross-cultural communication was also integral to earlier media: wampum, for instance, which recorded important historical alliances. Dramatic enactments were often associated with wampum. Augustine pointed out that documentation exists about a meeting in the first half of the nineteenth century, when two Maliseet from Tobique were asked to go the Mohawk community of Kahnawake to observe treaty making, including the final act of passing the wampum belt through fire before it formally represented an agreement between the two communities. Their role was not simply to accept the wampum, then, but to observe the ceremonies and be able to reenact them before their grand chief, Michael Augustine (from Elsipogtog), upon their return home. Song and dance performances were an important part of such transactions between First Nations, and treaty making facilitated the sharing of these traditions, among other forms of knowledge.

While it is different to learn by doing, to watch and listen rather than read about something, indigenous ways of knowing should not be reductively described as exclusively oral traditions. On the other hand, the dangers of articulating anything about traditional indigenous knowledge in print are precisely the limitations of print itself. Print is fixed. While contemporary scholars have attempted to write in ways that do not totalize knowledge, that acknowledge context and social circumstance, print is not the best medium for conveying the flow and flux, the contingencies, and the rich detail contained in traditional ways of knowing. Stephen Augustine emphasizes that it is oral transmission, including singing, that has sustained traditional knowledge, thus making the very process of transmission integral to the development of Native American modernity.

TRADITIONAL INDIGENOUS KNOWLEDGE

In the late twentieth century, there was a subtle shift in the discourse from "traditional ways of knowing" to "traditional indigenous knowledge," from discussion of process to the identification of a distinctive body of knowledge that indigenous communities maintain and use. Many of the pressures on indigenous people to name and define indigenous knowledge relate to urgent concerns resulting from threats from outsiders. Indigenous knowledge of plants and natural materials is now sought by chemical and pharmaceutical companies. Images are used indiscriminately as logos and trademarks without compensation to the indigenous owners. Ecotourism infringes on space that has been used for ceremonial purposes, and land claims remain in dispute in most areas. In relation to traditional song repertoires, questions of access and ownership are similarly important and difficult issues to resolve within the narrow definitions of such legal mechanisms as "copyright." Differences in understanding need to be articulated before they may be resolved. For reasons such as these, indigenous people are pressured to identify specific localized forms of indigenous knowledge as well as to recognize commonalities between ways of knowing in different indigenous communities, not just in North America but around the world.

The TIK label is a recent product of the late twentieth century. While it has helped to get wider acknowledgement of the struggles described in the previous paragraph, and has thus been useful, it is simultaneously problematic. In the singular, it implies a homogeneous body of knowledge that is old and static. If used in the plural, however, it denies the deep resonances between different localized ways of knowing in indigenous communities.

Another thing about the TIK label about which you should be wary is its widespread appropriation. It may be used in a confusing manner, as a vague index of morality or spirituality, for instance. Oversimplified or generalized descriptions of traditional knowledge abound and they often feed into new stereotypes, associated with New Age spiritual traditions. TIK sells. Its imagery and generalized ideas are used on jewelry, T-shirts, TV commercials, and in many other forms. Indeed, as Sadie Buck said in our initial conversation about this book, "Traditional knowledge is a buzzword." So, the challenge is to consider carefully not only the sources that claim to define traditional indigenous knowledge, but the conditions from which these sources emerged. Who claims TIK and for what purposes?

THE GREAT TEXTS OF NATIVE AMERICAN COMMUNITIES AS TIK?

Every First Nation and Inuit tradition has a number of classic oral narratives that embody fundamental beliefs about cosmology, social life, values, and relationships. These are significant starting points in our endeavor to understand TIK. Nonetheless, it is impossible to understand worldview with such a brief overview of these rich teachings. As Sadie Buck said when she read a draft of this chapter, "In order to understand, students must do way more work and have a huge level of commitment."

In most cases the "great texts" of Native Americans are legends, although the word for legend in some languages may be the same as the word for prophecy, or history. Many First Nations, the Haudenosaunee among them, recognize a creation story. Even where there is not such a category, there may be a particular word to distinguish classic narratives from other kinds of stories, as is the case with many nations that speak languages of the Algonquian language family. The Innu, for instance, make a distinction between *atnuhana* (classic legends) and *tipat-shimuna* (stories), although all are regarded as true and important. The Mi'kmaq make a similar distinction between *a'tukan* (best kept stories; information that has always been around) and *agnutmakan* (news, more recent information). As with the Innu and Mi'kmaq, there is no single Inuit creation story but rather there are some widely known legends that describe many different interactions between Inuit and the natural/spiritual worlds in which they live. To learn how to pronounce the words in different indigenous languages in this text, see the online language dictionaries in the Resources list.

How exactly does an oral performance of a narrative embody traditional indigenous knowledge? It may teach the importance of regularly renewing a relationship with Creation—the seasons, the gifts of the earth, the social relationships. The context of the telling may be important for this reason. In some communities, certain stories are told only at certain times of year. In this regard, legends are like ceremonies. The Green Corn Ceremonies described briefly in Chapter 3 or the annual cycle of Longhouse "doings" of the Haudenosaunee discussed in Chapter 4 are an enacting of the relationship between people and the annually unfolding gifts of Creation.

Legends may encourage listeners to use their minds and to make ethical decisions for themselves. The meaning of these narratives is neither fixed nor always clear. As Stephen Augustine said, in European stories the "moral" closes the book and people don't have to think anymore, but in Native stories, there is no ending and you have to think about what it means (2005). In relation to the examples below, the activities suggested may require independent thinking. You may be asked to observe what can be learned from one animal or another. You may also feel more sympathy for one than another. If you are asked whether you like the ptarmigan or snow bunting better in the Inuit legend discussed below (CD track 1), there is no right answer, but your decision may tell you whether you like patience more than persistence, or vice versa. In relation to the Haudenosaunee Thanksgiving Address, you are asked to contemplate what one repeated phrase, "Let it be so in our minds," might mean. One of the prepublication readers of this textbook asked, "How can the students answer this?" The fact that there is no right answer is the point. Your individual answer will tell you something about your own views of community and your attitudes toward individualism.

Legends teach us that accidental and unexpected incidents in our lives are important teachings. Such incidents also make us laugh, and as Anishnabe playwright Drew Hayden Taylor has written, "Humour is the WD-40 of healing" (2005, 70). This is the essence of the concept of the "trickster," a shape-changing character with many names in different communities. He/she is a character who teases everyone and is particularly adept at making fun of himself/herself. His/her bawdy humor may be politically incorrect but it is joyous and celebratory. Trickster-like elements may be found in stories below and in song traditions discussed in other chapters (the Haudenosaunee *E̜hsgá:nye:* for instance). However, we should also heed Stephen Augustine's dislike of the term "trickster," as explained below. His preference for "culture hero" suggests the need to be sensitive to local aesthetics as we explore several specific examples of the classic texts.

The Mi'kmaq have no single creation story, although they do have a category of *gisu'lq*, which means "you have been made; creation is unfolding." As Augustine explains, the Mi'kmaq creation story (Figure 1.5) is "not shared wholly but given out in bits and pieces," some about animals, winds, the culture hero Kluskap, and the seven levels of creation. Many of these Mi'kmaq stories were written down by the Baptist missionary Silas Rand in the early twentieth century. Since Rand's time, "Kluskap" has been spelled in many different ways: an anglicized form, "Glooscap," is among them. The name derives from the word *kelulesgub* ("*kl'gescap*," meaning "the first who spoke"). The character has been described variously as a "person who tells a lot of lies," and even "a cross between Christopher Columbus and Jesus Christ." Literary critics often refer to him as a "trickster," but while he has a good sense of humor like many of the trickster figures of other nations, Augustine prefers to call him a "culture hero," which in his view conveys that Kluskap has the "softer, subtler qualities that characterize the Mi'kmaq worldview." He elaborates by noting that the Mi'kmaq presence on the land is also subtle and often imperceptible, reflecting the belief that the people belong to the land, not the land to the people. "There are no totem poles or permanent houses in Mi'kmaq communities," he observes. The stories reflect the same worldview as the material culture.

Stories are often not separable from song and dance traditions. Augustine explains, for instance, that the Mi'kmaq *Neskweduk*, a "welcoming dance," is a part of the creation story since its lopsided dance step is a means of "announcing the self to Mother Earth." A legend, then, may be performed with movement and song, as well as with spoken words. In recent decades, the great legends have been maintained by puppet troupes, playwrights, musicians, dancers, and filmmakers (A Haudenosaunee instance of this is discussed below). Renewing the *way* they are performed has been an important means of transmitting traditional teachings to new generations.

Like the Mi'kmaq, the Inuit have no single creation story but a number of legends that expand upon the relationship of humans, animals, and environment. One of these is the legend of "The Ptarmigan and the Snow Bunting" (CD track 1).

The grandmother who was too tired to tell her granddaughter a story and then frightened her, the resultant dismay over the transformation of the little girl into a snow bunting, and the gradual transformation of the grandmother into a ptarmigan intrigue us. What qualities of the two birds are conveyed in the story? What emotions are symbolized? How do the vocal qualities of the narrator enact the transformation between human and bird life?

MI'KMAQ CREATION STORY
Narration by Stephen Augustine

Kisu'lk

Kisu'lk (gee-soolg) is the one who made everything. Sometimes *Kisu'lk* is referred to as *Kji Niskam* (Jee nis-gam), or the Great Spirit. Neither word implies gender, because it is not important whether the Great Spirit is a he or a she.

The Mi'kmaq people do not explain how the Great Spirit came into existence, only that Creator is responsible for everything being where it is today. Creator made everything.

Naku'set

Naku'set (nah-goo-set) is the sun which travels in a circle and owes its existence to Creator. *Naku'set* is the giver of life. It is also a giver of light and heat. The power of *Naku'set* is held with much respect among the Mi'kmaq and other aboriginal peoples.

The Creation of Wsitqamu'k

Wsitqamu'k (oo-sit-gah-moo) is the Earth, or the area of land upon which the Mi'kmaq people walk and share its abundant resources with the animals and plants. *Wsitqamu'k* refers to the Mi'kmaq world which encompasses all the area where the Mi'kmaq people can travel or have traveled upon.

Wsitqamu'k was created by Creator and was placed in the centre of the circular path of *Naku'set*, the sun. *Naku'set* was given the responsibility of watching over the Mi'kmaq world. *Naku'set* shines bright light upon *Wsitqamu'k* as it passes around its path, and this brought the days and nights.

The Creation of Kluskap

After the Mi'kmaq world was created and after the animals, birds and plants were placed on the surface, Creator caused a bolt of lightning to hit the surface of *Wsitqamu'k*. This bolt of lightning caused the formation of an image of a human body. It was Kluskap (gloos-cap), first shaped out of the basic element of the Mi'kmaq world, sand.

Creator unleashed another bolt of lightning which gave life to Kluskap, but he could not yet move. He was stuck to the ground, watching the world go by and *Naku'set* travel across the sky everyday. His head was facing the direction of the rising sun, his feet were in the direction of the setting sun, his right hand was pointed North, and his left hand was in the South direction.

Kluskap watched the animals, the birds and the plants grow and pass around him. He asked *Kisu'lk* to give him freedom to move about the Mi'kmaq world. So it was that a third blast of lightning came, and that caused Kluskap to become free and to be able to stand on the surface of the Earth.

After Kluskap stood up on his feet, he turned around in a full circle seven times. He then looked toward the sky and gave thanks to Creator for giving him life. He looked down and gave thanks to *Wsitqamu'k* for offering its sand for his creation. He looked within himself and gave thanks to *Kisu'lk* for giving him his soul and spirit. Kluskap then gave thanks to the four directions, starting in the direction of sunrise, and following the sun: East, South, West and North. In all he gave his heartfelt thanks to the seven directions.

Kluskap then went out to explore *Wsitqamu'k*, to see what he might earn about where he lived. He traveled in the direction of the setting sun, until he came to an ocean. He then went South until the land narrowed, and he could see two oceans on either side. He journeyed back to where he started from, and then continued towards the North, to the land of ice and snow. Finally, he came back to the East, where he decided to stay, because it was where he came into existence. He again watched the animals, the birds and the plants. He watched the water and the sky. Creator taught him to watch and learn about the world. Kluskap watched but he did not disturb the world around him. He finally asked Creator to tell him the purpose of his existence. He was told that he would meet someone soon.

[To read other sections of the Mi'kmaq Creation Story (The Coming of Nukumi, The Coming of Netawansum, The Coming of Ni'kanaptekewi'skwm, Kluskap's Life, Kluskap's Departure and Final Teachings as told by Stephen Augustine, see http://www.muiniskw.org/pgCulture3a.htm]

- story adapted from "Mi'kmaq Knowledge in the Mi'kmaq Creation Story: Lasting Words and Deeds," by Stephen Augustine, April 8, 1977

FIGURE 1.5 *A portion of the Mi'kmaq creation story as narrated by Stephen Augustine.* *(Used with permission.)*

What can we learn from this story? Immediately it is apparent that the worlds of humans and animals are interrelated, that they sometimes mirror one another, and that beings may change shape from one thing to another in certain circumstances. We learn that beings observe one another very carefully and find ways to negotiate their fears and their obligations.

ACTIVITY 1.4 *How would you describe the changes of vocal timbre that the narrator uses in the context of this legend?*

In Haudenosaunee culture, there are many variants of the creation story, some elements of which have become widely known beyond the local community. You may have heard North America referred to as "Turtle Island," for instance. This designation comes from an early part of the story in which a woman falls through a hole in the sky into a world below. She lands on the back of a turtle. An otter dives to the bottom of the sea and brings up some earth to place on the turtle's back. The woman dances on that earth and, as she does so, the turtle as well as the soil begin to grow. As the story unfolds, the woman plants the "three sisters"—corn, beans, and squash—which will sustain her people. She gives birth to twin boys who embody aspects of good and evil (although sometimes it is hard to tell which is which) and who will eventually rule over the night and day.

The Haudenosaunee have other great texts that one might look to as teachings about traditional knowledge, codices that outline their system of government, their customs and values. One elder, the late Reginald Henry, created a chart (Figure 1.6) that indicates the historical sequence of these teachings, each one a point of renewal.

The oldest of these texts is the Great Law of Peace, brought by a messenger from the Creator who was from the Huron nation. He is often referred to as the Peacemaker or the fatherless man (although the "fatherless man" on the chart above may also be interpreted as a Christian reference to Jesus). An English-language version of the Great Law was recorded and made publically available by the late Confederacy chief Jake Thomas. He explains:

> To the Iroquois, peace was the law. They used the same word for both. Peace (the Law) was righteousness in action, the practice of justice between individuals and nations. If they ever recognized it as a mystic presence, like the light which Shelley conceived as giving

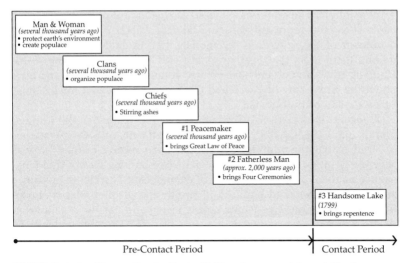

FIGURE 1.6 *Cayuga linguist Reginald Henry's representation of Haudenosaunee history. (Chart by Reginald Henry. Used by permission of the Woodland Cultural Centre, Brantford, Ontario.)*

"grace and truth to life's unquiet dream," they found it, not in some imagined retreat from the world, but in human institutions, especially in a good government. Their own Confederacy, which they named the Great Peace, was sacred. The chiefs who administered the League were their priests. (Iroquoian Institute, 1990)

The Peacemaker's teachings outlined the structure of the Confederacy of Five (later Six) Nations as a metaphorical longhouse, with the Onondaga as the firekeepers, the Mohawk and Seneca nations as the eastern and western doors, respectively, and the Cayuga and Oneida nations next to them. He explained a decision-making process that would allow the people of all nations to live in peace, power, and righteousness. The obligations and moral responsibilities of the fifty *sachems,* or Confederacy Council members—symbolized in a wampum design—as well as of the clan mothers were also given at this time. While women did not sit on the Council, the clan mothers were responsible for choosing Council members. The Peacemaker used the image of a giant white pine tree with roots extending in each of the four directions, signifying outreach to all mankind. The branches symbolized shelter and protection, and an eagle at the top represented seeing far. The Peacemaker also brought a number of the important ceremonies that are still practiced today, among them the Great Feather Dance and Peach Stone Game. Some Iroquois artists and elders have created contemporary images and texts about the Great Law of Peace and the Tree of Peace. See, for instance, http://sixnations.buffnet.net.

A second important text for Haudenosaunee people is the Code of Handsome Lake, *Gaihwí:yo* (also spelled *Gai'wiio*, or *Gaiwiio*) a series of visions that the prophet Handsome Lake received when he was severely ill in 1801. This was a time of distress among the six Haudenosaunee nations, largely as a result of colonialism. The Haudenosaunee suffered land loss, and endured ill health and alcohol-related abuses due to colonization. Handsome Lake's vision and narrow escape from death represented a renewal of many principles established by the Great Law. The Code established the Longhouse religion as it is practiced to the present day.

A third oral narrative that permeates Haudenosaunee thinking is *Ganǫ́hǫnyǫhk*, the Thanksgiving Address. This "speech" is offered at the beginning of every community event. It may take five minutes or ninety, depending on the narrator and the circumstances, but its basic form is always the same, as Michael Foster (1974) has described. It acknowledges all parts of creation, starting from the beings of the waters and below the earth, to all who move the earth, to the sky worlds, the winds, and finally to Handsome Lake. After each segment giving thanks to the specific energies and beings within the hierarchy, the narrator speaks a phrase that is often translated "This is the way it should be in our minds." The fundamental obligation to give thanks as a means of keeping balance among the complementary energies in the world underlies Haudenosaunee dance and song traditions, as discussed further in Chapter 4.

ACTIVITY 1.5 *Write a short essay about what the phrase "This is the way it should be in our minds" implies to you. Compare your thoughts with those of different members of your class. Does it suggest, for example, that all who hear the Thanksgiving Address should think the same way? Does it indicate that an attitude of gratitude and respect can underlie independent thinking? Or is there some other implication?*

The Thanksgiving Address continues to play a role in modern artistic creations. An example is the dance drama *Kaha:wi* created by Mohawk Santee Smith (Figure 1.7, CD track 2). She incorporates the voice of elder Gordie Buck delivering the *Ganǫhǫnyǫhk* in the last five minutes of an electronic composition entitled "Life Force," the first section of the dance drama. In this way, she honors the tradition of beginning a ceremony or social event with thanksgiving, simultaneously creating an evocative new context using electronic sounds and modern choreography. Her work is a compelling instance of the way traditional knowledge continues to inform indigenous modernity.

FIGURE 1.7 *Santee Smith and partner dancing in Kaha:wi.* *(Photograph by Cylia Von Tiedman. Photo courtesy of Santee Smith.)*

Narratives, of course, are not the only places to look if one seeks to understand traditional knowledge. The way in which the gifts of Creation are used is another. The lifeways, beliefs, and experiences of individuals are the manifestations of that.

Not all teachings about traditional knowledge are old. A significant recognition of traditional knowledge as process is in the post-1999 Nunavut government's documents on "Inuit Qaujimajatuqangit" (often abbreviated strategically as "IQ"). A close translation of "*qaujimajatuqangit*" is "those things that have been known for a long time," but the emphasis is on "process," not "things." Jaypeetee Arnakak, writing for *Nunatsiaq News,* describes the challenge of defining Inuit Qaujimajatuqangit:

> The question itself is like asking how many grains of sand there are on Baffin Island. We can never hope to count each and every single grain of sand, but we can describe what a grain of sand generally looks like… In fact, IQ is a living technology. It is a means of rationalizing thought and action, a means of organizing tasks and resources, a means of organizing family and society into coherent wholes . . . It is a set of teachings on practical truisms about society, human nature and experience passed on orally (traditionally) from one generation to the next; It is the knowledge of country that covers weather patterns, seasonal cycles, ecology, wildlife, use of resources, and the interrelationships of these elements; It is holistic, dynamic and cumulative in its approach to knowledge, teaching and learning—that one learns best by observing, doing and experience. (Arnakak 2000, online)

Nunavut government documents define five processes that embody Inuit Qaujimajatuqangit. They are *pijitsirarniq* (serving), *aajiiqatigiingniq* (decision making), *ilimmaksarniq* (knowledge acquisition), *qanuqtuurungnarniq* (being resourceful to solve problems), *piliriqatigiingniq* (working together for a common purpose), and *avatimik kamattiarniq* (environmental stewardship). Of course, governments have agendas that may differ from those of the elders who articulate these processes. Some feel that governments are a source of conflict in indigenous communities, and they mistrust government uses of language that describe traditional ways of knowing. One of my Aboriginal advisors suggests that when the language of TIK is used by authorities, it is an example of "cognitive dissonance," which social psychologists define as the incompatibility between different forms of knowledge (Festinger 1957). At the very least, it is important to know what informs our knowledge and for what purposes institutions appropriate specific language.

Nonetheless, there are some comparable aspects of traditional knowledge in the belief systems of different Native American groups and these echo some of the principles outlined as Inuit Qaujiman-gatuqangit. These include:

• the importance of place and keen attention to the environment, including environmental sound and the properties of natural materials used for sound production

• the significance of oral transmission as a means of passing knowledge from one generation to another, sometimes by means of carefully defined kinship networks

• the centrality of participation and experience; secondhand knowledge is less authoritative, as mentioned earlier

• the relationality of all knowledge, including an awareness of the authority of the speaker and his or her connections to other beings

Several of these issues have particular relevance for the study of sound and song. Our challenge here, however, like the one Jaypeetee describes, is to avoid generalizations, since when elders speak of traditional knowledge, it is often very detailed and specific. In order to try to explore how concepts of traditional knowledge shape cultures of hearing and singing, the remainder of this chapter will focus on some very specific examples relating to the principles stated above. One principle precedes them all, and that is the way in which language shapes worldview and "worldhearing."

LANGUAGE, ORAL TRANSMISSION, AND WORLDVIEW

All of our global universe will hinge in the next century on how we respect each other. In another language such as English which reflects a noun consciousness and more "tions" than verb words, we begin to see how different the reflection of philosophy is that exists between the Aboriginal perspective and the non-Aboriginal perspective.

(M. Battiste 1997, 148)

Imagine, if you will, two English-speaking people coming out of a movie. The first says "Boy, that was a depressing movie!" The second says, "Boy, was that an inspiring movie!" It is almost as if they believe the movie "is" something all by itself. As a result, it seems perfectly reasonable to argue about who has characterized it "correctly"

> *and who has missed the mark…When I am with Aboriginal people,*
> *however, I keep hearing a different way of exchanging information. The*
> *first might say, "Boy, I feel depressed after seeing that movie," follow-*
> *ing which the other laughs and says, "No kidding, I feel really inspired*
> *after seeing that movie!" After that they both chuckle about how differ-*
> *ently they were touched.*
>
> (Ross 1996/2006, 106)

Each language shapes and influences a view of the world. There are approximately eight hundred indigenous languages spoken in the western hemisphere. A good starting point for those who wish to learn more about them is www.native-languages.org (other language resources are listed in the Resources section of this book). By the turn of the twenty-first century, spelling systems (orthographies) are still locally variable. Hence, some of the spellings used in this textbook may not be the same as others you find. Variants have been indicated wherever possible.

The indigenous languages of people whose aural traditions are discussed in this book are from three entirely unrelated language families. A language family consists of different languages that share common origins and often have related vocabulary or grammatical constructions. In the cultures that are the focus of this textbook, Algonquian languages are the most numerous. Included in this language family are all the languages of Atlantic Canada—Beothuk, Mi'kmaq/Maliseet, and Innu—and many others from other regions not discussed in this volume, including Anishnabe, Cree, and Blackfoot. While some, such as Innu and Eastern Cree, may be mutually intelligible, other languages within the Algonquian language family, such as Innu and Mi'kmaq, are mutually unintelligible.

Most Inuit languages in Canada—including Inuttitut in Nunavik, Inuktitut in Nunavut, and Inuvialuktun in Inuvialuit—are interrelated but quite different from the Aleut and Yupik languages of Alaska, for instance. Furthermore, dialects may differ substantially from one another. Seven dialects of Inuktitut are spoken in Nunavut alone.

The six Haudenosaunee nations each have their own language. While all belong to the same language family and are mutually intelligible, singers comment on the distinctive rhythmic qualities of each. The Cherokee language, Tsalagi, also belongs to the Iroquoian language family.

Hearing each language is essential. Reference was made earlier to the online dictionaries listed under "Resources." The online Mi'kmaq site, www.mikmaqonline.org, is particularly useful, since words are pronounced and in some cases incorporated into sentences. There are also audio dictionaries for several Iroquois languages at www.ohwejagehka. com, although the vocabulary range is restricted at the time of writing. Good Inuktitut language resources may be accessed through the Nunavut Arctic College at www.nac.nu.ca.

Those of us who have studied one or more indigenous languages, but who do not speak those languages with fluency, often initially see starkly contrasted and rigid differences between indigenous languages and English. The "natural" and "cultural" domains are not so clearly distinguished in Native American languages, and neither are the "secular" and "sacred." These binary constructions are fundamental organizational principles in English. It is important to recognize that, in some indigenous formulations, concepts may not be polarized or even distinguished. In some Innu dialects, for instance, a drum may be an "animate" noun—indicating that it may have consciousness and hence some spiritual connotations—while a drumstick may be inanimate. But this linguistic marking is variable from one community to another. One type of berry might have spirit associations, but not every type of berry. Hence, the constructions are localized and not distinguished in a rigidly logical way. Where polarities exist, they may be defined differently in different communities.

It is useful to listen to the way the Inuit and First Nations advisors for this project, as well as other Native American intellectuals, speak about language and worldview. They share the insights that specific language competence gives them.

As Marie Battiste notes in the statement at the outset of this section, a major distinction between English and Aboriginal languages is the verb-based consciousness of the latter. She explains this eloquently with regard to Mi'kmaq.

> Mi'kmaq is a verb-based language which focuses on the processes, cycles and interrelationships of all things. Unlike English and its related languages that are noun-based, Mi'kmaq identifies objects and concepts in terms of their use or their relationship to other things in an active process. Mi'kmaq language resonates the importance of relations and relationships, for these are important to our total survival. Mi'kmaq people believe that because all things are connected, all of us must depend on each other and help each other as a way of life, for that is what it means to be in balance and harmony with earth. (M. Battiste 1997, 148)

She explains that Mi'kmaq children may have trouble learning in mainstream schools where teachers are trained to develop language skills by first focusing on the concrete, the objects and nouns. This focus is at odds with the Mi'kmaq child's preschool education. Battiste's husband, Sakej Henderson (Chicksaw-Cherokee), taught Rupert Ross something similar, although Ross stressed orality itself: "…when you're speaking Mi'kmaq, you can go all day long *without saying a single noun.* My eyes can see nouns…That's what my eyes are supposed to do, see nouns, and obstacles and tracks and trails. But that's not what the function of the language is. It's not to become another pair of eyes. It's supposed to be speaking to the ear and to the heart…" (Ross 2006, 114).

Henderson describes how things are named in terms of their relationship to their surroundings. In Mi'kmaq, trees are "called by the sounds that are made as the wind goes through their branches, in the autumn, during a special period just before dusk" (in Ross, 120).

The aural and visual are interrelated. This relationship has implications for the transmission of music and the teaching of musical skills. In community contexts, children are expected to learn by observing adults at work. Inuit Karin Kettler, who describes herself as a visual learner, commented that she learned throat singing by looking at the neck and face of elders performing. Similarly, I know several young indigenous guitarists who learned Western harmony by looking closely at the finger placement on the fret board. Careful observation and hearing were equally important aspects of the transmission process.

The emphasis on process and interconnection is a characteristic of each of the Native American languages referred to in this book. Haudenosaunee singer Sadie Buck has explained that she does not think of herself as a "composer" but rather as one who "makes songs." Uttering a word evokes for her a long history and she hears "respect in the voice."

Karin Kettler says something similar about Inuktitut. When her son refers to her as "*anana*" (mother), she hears "an intimate relationship that you can only have with your son or daughter," a relationship that further indicates respect for her and for the culture they share. "People hearing this will know right away what the relationship is between them," she tells me. She returns his beckoning with "Yes, *irniq*" (son). This helps explain why story and song are powerful forms of social action. To sing a short personal song for a loved one, as in the Inuit *aqausit* tradition, is to take this quality of respect in the voice still further. The song may characterize or even protect its dedicatee. Respect for all creatures is apparent in the lyrics of songs. We will see how Inuit drum dances, for instance, avoid direct naming of animals but describe them indirectly, out of respect.

Like a number of other nonindigenous ethnomusicologists, I have often told my students that there are no words in most Native American languages for "music." In other words, "music" is a noun that fails to convey the processes and relationships that singing and drumming embody in many Native American contexts. It is also interesting that I and others have needed to discuss this translation matter in the classroom as if it was really problematic that *my* concept was not relevant. What was it, then, that I tried to research and teach as analogous to music, if "music" did not exist? This very question, which I have indeed asked in several communities, presupposes at least two things. One is the problematic assumption that whatever is analogous to music is separable from other things and that it should be studied as an entity in itself. The other is the faulty presupposition that "translation" was indeed necessary to understand.

> **ACTIVITY 1.6**   *Conduct a research project to explore two different concepts: "music" and "sound." (1) Find out how many different languages are spoken in your classroom. Compare words that are related to the concept of "music" and try to distinguish differences between them. Do any of your classmates speak a language that has no word for music? (2) What words can you think of for "sound"? Do the words you collect help you understand concepts within which singing and dancing may have a meaningful place?*

The discussion above indicates that approaches to teaching are culturally variable, of course. Sadie Buck thinks carefully about how to get her students to think outside of the mindset that English requires. She has them learn the orthography used for the Cayuga language and translate English phrases into that system: "Tai mai su" is clearly "Tie my shoe," in Cayuga orthography.

Aboriginal speakers including Buck frequently use puns or map old concepts onto new objects to communicate. The name for the radio station CKRZ in Sadie's community, for instance, means "it sings." Wordplay may be witty and funny. Read a play by Tomson Highway or Drew Hayden Taylor if you need convincing. Hayden Taylor's anthology of native humor equally reveals the qualities of language play that my advisors speak about. Native humor is often self-deprecating, but its puns play on the stereotypes that circulate in mainstream society and turn them in new directions. Have you heard the one about: "Two

Indians walked into a bar. Gee, you'd think one of them would have ducked" (2005, 132).

Another closely related quality of indigenous languages that Aboriginal collaborators emphasize is their polysemic potential. Depending on context and on the experience of the listeners, words can mean different things. In the Mi'kmaq language, Stephen Augustine uses the word "copious" to describe the nuances of a single word. He notes that good Mi'kmaq speakers like "language smithing"—playing with words, using them in new contexts as a means of "interaction with the world as it is alive today."

Perhaps most importantly, Stephen Augustine notes that his language is "conciliatory." There are no words for war, for aggression. He explains that even scolding is often done indirectly. He tells a story of his grandmother confronting a young person who had done something she shouldn't have; rather than chide her, his grandmother simply asked why she thought she found it necessary to do the action in question. She inspired careful reflection, not guilt. His comments suggest why it is important to emphasize encounter in the representation of First Nations along the Atlantic seaboard. As the first Native Americans to deal with European colonizers, they already had a language that enabled them to negotiate.

Sophisticated ways of expressing conciliation undoubtedly enabled First People in eastern North America to adapt new ideas and traditions from foreign visitors. Consider, for instance, how Christianity was indigenized by various communities. At the same time, First Nations and Inuit leaders were ever vigilant about why certain decisions were made, certain beliefs adopted. The question of "why" is considered in this textbook in relation to contemporary popular music (in Chapter 5). The ways in which these new musical forms have been used—at times to present a new historical perspective, at times to celebrate unsung heroes, at times to address current social issues, at times to build pride and have fun—will resonate with Augustine's story.

PLACE AND ATTENTION
TO THE ENVIRONMENT

Indigenous knowledge is bound to the knowledge of place and environment. Lakota author Vine Deloria Jr. makes a fundamental distinction between Native American and European approaches to time and place, arguing that Native Americans base their religions on place and largely discount time while the Christianity of Europeans focuses on time and discounts place (discussed in Rollings 2002, 133). While his words come from the western part of the continent, rather than from the communities of the north and east explored in this text, they resonate in all parts of Native America.

Stephen Augustine spoke with me extensively about Mi'kmaq attention to place and related this to sound and song. On one hand, he emphasized the practicality of choosing a place to live. His ancestors were basket makers and chose to live near groves of the specific type of ash tree needed for their craft. They also positioned themselves near a railway line so that their products could get to market. On the other hand, he spoke about the keen attention to the sonic environment, an attention that impacts Native music in a number of ways.

> One of the things that intrigues a lot of people—that I find strange— is [songs from indigenous people in other parts of the world, whether Africa, Scandinavia, or wherever] having similar beats and rhythms to [indigenous music in] North America. I've heard San and Navajo—music of the sand or desert. I've noticed you hear certain desert insects...I've been in New Mexico; there is one desert insect that is going [making a sound] the same way [as in South Africa]. It's not that these two societies are linked but there may be something similar in their environment. Even among ocean people, you hear the water and the crashing of the waves. You hear that differently at different times. Humans are mirroring those sounds, the repetitions and rhythms.

Our conversation returned to rhythm quite often. The symmetry of Mi'kmaq design and the repetition of arc-like patterns have a rhythm not unlike ocean waves, Stephen notes. But he is also careful to differentiate the sound and motion that vary from one place to another and one day or even hour to another. I am reminded of a comment I heard previously about the mirror image of the double curve design, an image that is prevalent in Mi'kmaq quill or beadwork, such as you see on this photo of a peaked hat (Figure 1.8), a style preferred by women in the eighteenth and nineteenth centuries. The single design is shaped like a canoe, the double one like a canoe and its reflection in the water. Which is real and which is reflection?

Stephen emphasizes that the Mi'kmaq language expresses very precise detail about the natural world: "The color of water, the texture of water, the surface of water, the salinity of water, the clarity of water. There's a lot of description of nature." Music, like language, has this capacity for detailed observation. At the same time, something is often

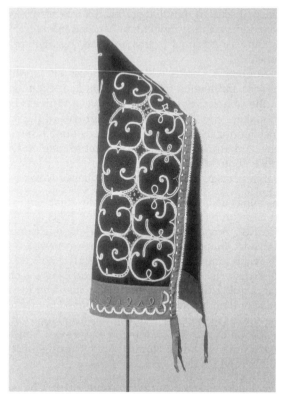

FIGURE 1.8   *Mi'kmaq peaked cap, late 19th century, 1875–1900. M101.*   *(Courtesy McCord Museum, Montreal)*

added when humans imitate other natural sounds. Stephen's words remind me of those of John Newell, a Mi'kmaq from Pictou Landing who told Wilson Wallis the following in 1911:

> One old Indian listened to the gull until it had finished its song. Thus he learned its song, and said to the others: "If you people care to dance to it, dance. If not, then merely listen to me." He then took a stick and beat time. But as he sang he wanted to put some words into the tune. He was thinking about a woman who was hunting for something, and accordingly he sang about this. (Wallis and Wallis 1955, 118–119)

Song as a mirror of nature is an idea that emerges in Inuit culture as well. In particular, the throat singing tradition imitates the sounds of the natural and, in some cases, also the man-made environment, as discussed in Chapter 2. In view of the fact that even very young Inuit children develop a keen ear for new environmental sounds, such as the motor noise of different makes of snowmobiles, it will be interesting to see whether these become sources for new vocal games in the future. Karin Kettler emphasizes another relationship to place, however. Some of the throat songs are associated with particular places, and she stresses that this knowledge needs to be carefully preserved.

Her comments remind me of similar comments by Sadie Buck, who has suggested that vocal timbres might be mapped, more generally, onto the different First Nations of North America. You can hear the sound of the place in the voices from there. With reference to the Aboriginal Women's Voices project, which she directed at the Banff Centre for the Arts in the late 1990s, she said, "We learned those songs [that each woman brought] and got each other used to knowing those sounds, their sound that they have from their region." To allow each timbre and style to be heard clearly, different women in turn take the lead on the "Travelling Song" (CD track 3) that they composed together in the course of the project.

ACTIVITY 1.7 *Listen to the "Travelling Song" (CD track 3), paying particular attention to the different vocal qualities and to the subtle stylistic differences between each of the lead singers. If you were a poet, how would you describe each voice?*

Sadie emphasizes that local knowledge must be taught with the song: "If it's sung in a certain way or if it's sung at a particular time, or if only certain people sing that, or if it's only sung with certain instruments, then you maintain that." But Sadie is wary of simply describing the sources of sounds. She worries that outsiders "see something and think it's one thing but that's not the *intent*." The "intent" of the singers, then, is inseparable from the meaning of the song.

Sadie has also described elsewhere how she sings in cooperation with the environment, not in spite of it. She pays attention to the voices in her own group of singers, ensuring that a strong voice is placed opposite another strong voice for balance, but also valuing the differences among them. She describes the slight differences in timbre and tuning when they sing in unison as their sort of "harmony." She is also aware of air flow, outdoors or in, and how that changes the sound of her voice.

Compare this approach with that of teachers in a Western music school. In choral singing, Sadie's approach contrasts markedly. Classical choirs espouse an ideal of "blended" sound rather than one in which the individuality of voices is cherished and used.

Classical voice teachers, on the other hand, discuss the solo human voice in a way that resonates in some ways and digresses in others from the concept Sadie Buck articulated. I asked my colleague, soprano Dr. Jane Leibel, whether she had an idealized sound in mind when she taught voice. She said that she endeavors to develop "the student's most efficient sublime sound," emphasizing that there is no cookie cutter, that the sound must reflect the way the person speaks or "phonates." She does, however, prefer a certain technique, the *bel canto* technique, because it enables a person to produce the clear sound required for classical performance, including opera. Dr. Leibel, who enjoys thinking about a range of cross-cultural issues, acknowledges that a different technique might be suitable for other repertoire, but she fears that other techniques would alter the vocal physique. "If I were diagnosed with nodules, I would flip out. I would totally wig out because you lose range, you lose your top. But what you get, you gain different colors and timbres and metallics" (personal communication, 2006). Her comments relate to the fact that "nodules," or thickened vocal folds, are problematic for classical singers. Her comments lead me to question, however, whether our ideas about the very health of the body depend on the way we map cultural constructs onto the body. Jane Leibel is acquainted with certain Native American approaches, having witnessed the supportive environment for singers when adjudicating in the Aboriginal communities of Labrador and noting the "energy and passion" of our local drum group. Her comments and her openness suggest to me that a huge area for fruitful investigation lies in the comparison of the ways teachers from different cultural traditions think about the human voice, about how to develop it in a healthy way and to train it for specific types of repertoire.

ACTIVITY 1.8 *Discuss with singers you know what their concepts of an ideal voice are and what they think about when they consider the "health" of the human voice. If possible, try to involve singers from different cultural traditions in this conversation. Where do their ideas resonate and where do they diverge?*

THE INSEPARABILITY OF TRADITIONAL INDIGENOUS KNOWLEDGE, ORAL TRANSMISSION, AND EXPERIENCE

Stephen Augustine emphasizes that oral transmission is the very reason that Native American cultures have survived. The passing on of narratives and songs is a responsibility that keeps them alive in memory and in practice.

Participants in an Inuit oral traditions project articulate a slightly different aspect of oral transmission. "Traditional knowledge is not something abstract and separated from the context in which it is produced, but is always related to the present," they write [Vol. I, 7; nac. nu.ca/online_publications]. They observe that "Inuit may have been even more literate than the average European country at the turn of the [twentieth] century," (I, 8) but that writing was used for Christianity, and practical matters such as letters, diaries, or accounting. They note that in Western society, truth was freed from the constraints of social relationships, and emphasize that Inuit believe "all knowledge is social by nature." Of course, many contemporary scholars in diverse cultural contexts share this view and critique the notion that any knowledge was ever autonomous.

The interconnection of perspectives is a priority in this book. The social process of dialogue between the author and Native American collaborators is not obscured but highlighted. The issue of song transcription was considered especially carefully. We tried to find ways to unfix visual representations of sound by comparing variants in some cases or by suggesting the limitations (as well as the advantages) of print.

By collaborating, we were able to be sensitive to different community views about access to certain recordings, transcriptions, and information. Concepts of access and ownership are often more nuanced in Native American systems of thought than in the laws of either Canada or the United States. Some song repertoires are understood to be the property of a family, a clan, a regional group, or a whole indigenous nation. Some repertoires are understood to be associated with (and hence only rightly performed in) a specific place. Some were gifts from one nation to another. The codification of customary laws about song transmission, access, and ownership have probably been developed the most extensively by Northwest Coast First Nations. In the far north and the east, the practices are more fluid and informal. An Inuit drum dance singer, for instance, would generally sing songs by members of his or her immediate family, and, before a song was performed (especially for an outsider), the singer might announce that "this song was made

by such and such a person, when they were doing such and such."
A singer is also at liberty to sing other songs, if desired.

When Sadie Buck taught my university students to make new Ęhsgá:nye
(a genre to be discussed in Chapter 4), she was careful to indicate that
these songs were a gift of the Creator to the Haudenosaunee nation and
were not to be performed in contexts other than Haudenosaunee ones.
The final assignment in her university course involved the whole class.
We had to organize and participate in a Haudenosaunee social. Community members also attended and danced while the class sang their
new repertoire. Then the class danced while community singers took
over. Their success in the course, then, was evident in their ability to
engage socially and participate appropriately.

Sadie again addressed the issue of sharing songs cross-culturally
when she developed the Aboriginal Women's Music program for the
Banff Centre for the Arts in the mid 1990s. Here, she insisted that women
exchange not simply songs, but also the stories about the songs. They
listened respectfully, before attempting to create new work together.

RELATIONALITY

The emphasis on oral transmission is tied to the inherently relational
nature of traditional knowledge. Relationship and reciprocity are emphasized in many contexts and in many ways in indigenous communities. In the aforementioned Inuit oral tradition project, Inuit discuss
"an essential feature of traditional knowledge; it is produced as an exchange" (I, 10; http://nac.nu.ca). Stephen Augustine explains that even
conflicts were mediated by reciprocity. While history books suggest that
the Mi'kmaq and Mohawk people were constantly at war, he thinks
there were more likely occasional rivalries and skirmishes between
families. He describes a Mi'kmaq / Mohawk custom whereby, when a
conflict had occurred, young girls from each nation were sent to live
with the "opponent" and vice versa. Hence, there was responsibility to
raise the daughters of your "enemy." The concept of balance emerged
frequently in conversation with Augustine.

Balance is similarly central to the political structure of the Haudenosaunee Confederacy, described metaphorically as a "longhouse." The
decision-making process involves all the nations coming to consensus
through a process in which nations to the east and west of the central
fire arrive at independent judgements and then share their views. The
Onondaga, as the central fire keepers, also discuss each issue and listen
to all sides, facilitating the emergence of consensus.

More directly related to music is the balance achieved through the annual ceremonial cycles of different nations, including the Green Corn Ceremonies of the Cherokee and Seminole in the Southeast (described briefly in Chapter 2) or the annual Longhouse cycle of the Haudenosaunees, described in Chapter 4. Here each song and dance is an integral means of giving thanks for each of the gifts of the Creator.

ACTIVITY 1.9 *The intent of this chapter is to look at how language, experience and lifeways, as well as classic narratives or other teachings shape the way sound, song, and dance are thought about in Native American cultures of the north and east. A few comparisons have been made with concepts and values encountered in Eurocentric music schools. (1) Make notes on ways in which your own experience of learning music has related to or differed from the processes of acquiring musical skills and knowledge discussed in this chapter. (2) Reread the chapter to see where words have, in spite of our best intentions, unjustly cast Native and non-Native ways of thinking as oversimplified opposites. Also note where the very process of writing in English may oversimplify complex and context-dependent (verb-oriented) processes as objectified (noun-oriented) facts.*

WHAT ETHNOMUSICOLOGY BRINGS
TO THE STUDY

Ethnomusicologists and their forefathers (many of whom called themselves "comparative musicologists") have been interested in Native American music cultures since the discipline began in the late nineteenth century. Many of their early initiatives were tied to the advent of audio recording technologies, and their motives were related to the salvaging of music that they feared would disappear with modernity. Jesse Fewkes's recording of Passamaquoddy Snake Dance songs, the song transcriptions by Carl Stumpf of a performance by Bella Coola, who toured in Berlin in 1885, Benjamin Gilman's Hopi recordings, Alexander Cringan's turn-of-the-century Iroquois wax cylinders, or the thousands of recordings made by Frances Densmore are some of the events within that audio history. Transcriptions by many of these early scholars may be found in Levine's *Writing American Indian Music: Historic Transcriptions, Notations, and Arrangements* (2002).

The objectives of ethnomusicological research, vis-à-vis Native Americans, have, of course, shifted, partly in response to the justifiable demands of communities that research be valuable on their terms. More recent ethnographers have asserted the vitality of contemporary cultures and countered the old Euro-American stereotype of Native American cultures as historically frozen in the past. Many of us, I would guess, would agree with Australian Tony Mitchell that "notions of musical purity and authenticity are an idealistic form of colonialist nostalgia" (1993, 335). But at the same time, we balance a profound respect for traditional teachings, including dance and song, with an admiration for the creative projects of innovative contemporary artists.

In recent decades, ethnomusicologists have emphasized processes and praxis (a word that combines two meanings: "accepted practice or custom" and the "practicing of an art or skill"). We have, for instance, often explored performance as part of an ongoing negotiation of indigenous identity in many localities worldwide. We seek to understand how that process of negotiation is shaped by its context. Consider just a few examples, some taken up in this volume and some listed in the Resources at the end. Tara Browner has unfolded how campus politics influenced one important powwow in Michigan. Michelle Bigenno has explored how South American indigenous musicians juggle the demands of tourist audiences, record producers, and local communities in their choices of outfit, repertoire, musical arrangement, and style of presentation. Richard Jones Bamman discusses how Saami musicians used their art to shift their self-definition from "I'm a Lapp" to "I'm a Saami." Karl Neuenfeldt has explored how beliefs and functions of the Australian didjeridoo have had to be renegotiated in light of the global popularity and Internet sales of this instrument. In another publication, I have considered Native American recordings as forms of social action, hence moving from an object approach to one that considers intent, production processes, and consumption patterns. Such initiatives bring ethnomusicology to a place where the indigenous emphasis on process is not at odds with the questions that scholars ask about Native American music.

In these ways, traditional indigenous knowledge about music has come to be discussed in ever-wider communities. Indigenous people worldwide are interested in sharing their teachings with one another. Academics change the very nature of their questions in order to engage in a meaningful conversation with community members and to understand the global processes that inflect all our lives.

CHAPTER 2

Music and Historical Encounter: Inuit Communities

While Chapter 1 explored some commonalities in the ways traditional indigenous knowledge has been approached and defined, it also stressed the importance of localized rather than generalized (and essentialized) observations and values. This chapter is the first of three that will examine music at the local and regional level.

The Inuit of Alaska, northern Canada, and Greenland have used songs, dances, games, and legends as forms of traditional knowledge that mediate their encounters with the land they occupy and the people who have come to it, both historically and in the present day. While Alaskan towns have a longer history, northern Canadian communities were in many cases quite isolated and ways of life changed rapidly only in the late twentieth century when government housing, schools, and Western medical services were introduced. More recently still, global communications media in the north have been significant influences, enabling Inuit modernity to develop in new ways. Music plays a role in bridging older nomadic hunting cultures and Inuit modernity.

Alongside First Nations and Métis, Inuit are one of three Aboriginal groups defined in the repatriated constitution of Canada in 1982. The ancestors of contemporary Inuit were international travellers who, from at least 2000 BCE, traversed the ice bridge that joined North America to Asia. Many Inuit think that there may have been travel back and forth between the continents. The map below shows the contemporary names for the regions that have the largest Inuit populations. In Canada there are four different regions with a majority Inuit population: the Territory of Nunavut, Nunavik (a region within Quebec), Nunatsiavut (a region within Newfoundland and Labrador), and the Inuvialuit Settlement Region of the Northwest Territories. Both "Regions" and "Territories" in Canada are self-governing, but their authority is defined somewhat differently from that of Provincial governments. These northern areas have been created at different times since the establishment of Nunavut in 1999. Inuit also use more localized names, adding the suffix "-miut" to a place to indicate they were people of that place. Places were sometimes named for the animals found in abundance there. Hence, the Netsilingmiut designated "people of the Netsilik region, and *"netsilik"* in turn means "seal." The Iglulingmiut lived in Iglulik, and so forth. Some of these names are also indicated on the map (Figure 2.1), since they occur later in this chapter. If you read ethnographies of Inuit, you will encounter regional names that anthropologists adopted. In many cases these conflate several different groups. The "Caribou" Inuit, for instance, consist of the Padliermiut, Ahiarmiut, and Sadliermiut, each with their own distinctive histories, beliefs, and customs.

Contemporary Inuit in Alaska speak Yupik or Aleut-related languages. Those in Nunavut, Nunavik, Inuvialuit, and Nunatsiavut speak variant dialects of Inuktitut, one of which we heard on CD track 1.

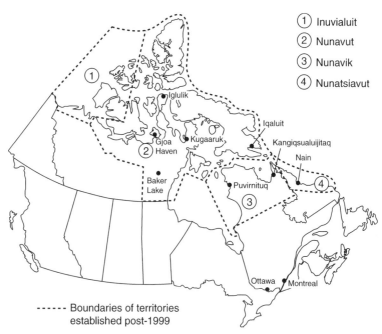

FIGURE 2.1   *Map of Inuit-dominant regions of Arctic Canada.*

Just as there are linguistic divergences, musical practices of western and eastern communities also differ. Their experiences of colonization differed, for one thing. Consider, for instance, the Moravian missions of Labrador, where music making was a very high priority. String ensembles and brass bands were maintained in the community of Nain until the late twentieth century. There was a tradition there of performing from the rooftop of the mission house (Figure 2.2), even during cold Arctic winters. Recent studies (Gordon 2006) demonstrate that, over time, the European styles were indigenized and new compositions were created by Inuit.

In the northeastern and western Arctic, where European whalers were frequent visitors to communities, the traditions of square dancing (typically in a large circle including everyone in the community) with accordion or fiddle accompaniment were often adopted. In northern Quebec, Inuit developed a string instrument with a trapezoid-shaped box resonator.

TRADITIONAL GENRES OF SONG

Not just the music influenced by colonizers, but also the precontact song and dance traditions of the north were regionally distinguished. In the Northwest Territories, as far east as the Mackenzie River and in Alaska, thin-framed drums are beaten with long willowy sticks. In communities in these western Arctic regions, mimetic story songs are performed by dancers wearing decorative gloves; masks, too, are in some instances essential dramatic regalia.

A larger drum (*qilaut*) with a much heavier wooden frame and handle is the instrument of drum dancers in Nunavut and has more recently also been reintroduced in Nunatsiavut. It is played solo, hit only on the drum frame by a thick drumstick wielded by a solo drum dancer. His dancing is accompanied by the singing of a chorus (often women) performing a personal, narrative song, often that of the dancer himself. In Greenland, a smaller variant of this handle-drum is widely used.

In contrast to the narrative drum dance repertoire, songs of other Inuit genres are relatively short. This chapter will describe games of various sorts: songs accompanying juggling and throat singing, which has now become internationally known. Other musical genres (not discussed extensively here) are *aqausit*, short songs of endearment made for loved ones, especially one's children, and some legends that include song in performance.

FIGURE 2.2 *Photo (a) of a coastal Labrador brass ensemble (probably from Nain) from the mid-20th century, with second inset photo (b), showing a performance from the roof of the mission building.* (E. Delaney album (V87–26.5 and V 87 27.1). Courtesy of the Provincial Archives of Newfoundland and Labrador.)

INUIT MUSIC AS HISTORICAL RECORD
AND JUDICIAL SYSTEM

As a means of preserving traditional knowledge, Inuit have continued to compose and perform narrative songs with drum accompaniment. Drum dance songs may be named variously in different regions. They are called *pisiit* (singular is *"pisiq"*) in many communities, although they are also known as *"ajaja"* songs, with reference to the vocables used in the refrains. These *pisiit* record local experiences, hence constituting a kind of historical record. They also articulate intense emotions and social tensions, and were traditionally used to mediate disagreements, serving as a sort of informal judicial system.

In Nunavut, the songs are most often carefully composed and privately rehearsed before they are presented at a drum dance. The line between "composition," "song reception," and "improvisation," however, is not rigid. One singer whom I recorded in the 1970s improvised a verse about the visiting woman who was collecting songs. Some songs are received in dreams or in that half-awake state one is in early in the morning after a night's sleep. Songs may remain static, or composers may add to a song when new experiences warrant a new verse.

While there is no rigid concept of song ownership, a singer will usually name the composer out of respect. Individual men and women make up songs about hunting, community life, and their travels on the land.

The Netsilingmiut (see map) have some of the most elaborated song narratives. In other regions, the text may be abbreviated, or absent altogether. Songs from western Greenland, for instance, use only vocables in performance, although singers may recall words as they sing those vocables. There is, in effect, a silent text that is in their minds but not made public.

Drum dances often took place in a dance space called a *qaggi* in many areas. When Nunavut people lived in snow houses, a large central dome was constructed, with smaller domes around the perimeter for individual families. Today, the school gymnasium or community center is a more likely meeting place for both traditional and contemporary dances, concerts, or public meetings.

While drum dances were traditionally held to welcome hunters home or to celebrate visitors arriving, there are now new types of events that feature drum dancing. The Arctic Winter Games is one such celebration, bringing people together from many different communities. They participate in competitions and demonstrations of drum dancing, traditional games, tea making in the snow, throat singing, and other northern activities.

What happens at a drum dance? In communities with the solo drum dancing tradition, the large frame drum, the *qilaut*, must first be tuned by tightening the membrane. Since drums are large, varying in size from two to three feet in diameter, they are awkward to tune. This is a slow process when caribou rawhide is used for the membrane, but various lighter materials, including plastic or synthetic fabrics, are now usually regarded as more convenient.

The solo drum dancer begins to turn the instrument from side to side, striking the frame on one side of the handle and then the other, creating two slightly different pitches and timbres. The slow turning of this large drum is graceful to watch. The sound is carried back and forth like a wave. The drummer (Figure 2.3) bends forward and flexes his or her knees with the drumbeats, slowly moving sideways in a circle or arc. While Figure 2.3 conveys something about the posture and motion of a good dancer, video is more effective in this regard (see Resources list). Considerable strength is needed to play this drum for the duration of a long narrative song.

The gendering of drum dancing differs from one community to another; in some cases, only men will play the drum, while women sing in the accompanying chorus. Women drum in some communities, however, and both boys and girls are being taught to drum in contemporary classes.

The form and melodic shape of a drum dance song make it a good vehicle for telling a story. A series of strophes are each framed by a "refrain" using the vocables *"ajaja."* (The "j" in Inuktitut is always pronounced like "y" in the English word "yet.") Hence the form is:

aja refrain – texted story – aja refrain

Either the vocable refrain itself or the final text line that leads back to the refrain usually has the most expansive melodic range. The middle part of the strophe, on the other hand, may have a series of phrases with many tone reiterations. This is the part where the story unfolds. There is not a regular meter, since the rhythm of the words dictates the number of "notes" in the phrase.

The Inuit Heritage Centre of Baker Lake has created an excellent website where performances of drum dances from that community can be heard and where song texts and translations are also posted. The website is called Tuhaalruuqtut Ancestral Sounds. Because URLs often change, the easiest way to locate the site is probably to enter "Tuhaalruuqtut" in your favorite search engine. It is simplest to enter the site using Interface 2 (HTML, static). Click "enter" to get to a page entitled

FIGURE 2.3 *Simon Keanik of Gjoa Haven drum dancing in 1973. (Photo by B. Diamond)*

"People, Shamans, and Spirits." There are one hundred "pages" in this collection and the location of each is in the top line (centered) of each slide, in the format "7 of 100," for instance. Slide 7 is labelled "Four Inuit men met by J. B. Tyrell." Slide 8 is labelled "Three Inuit men just arrived by qajait." Slide 9 is labelled "Inuit men on qajait." Each title refers to the image rather than the sound file(s) on the slide.

ACTIVITY 2.1 *Listen to the drum dances on pages 7 and 8 of the Tuhaalruuqtut site, following the text transcriptions carefully, until you can distinguish the texted strophes from the* "ajaja" *refrains. There is not always a break between the sections. The first refrain in each strophe is often abbreviated, sometimes to a single* "aja." *Note also that the breaks where the singer takes a breath may occur in the middle of a word, not always at the end of a phrase.*

The first song (#7) is a cheerful one sung by three women about a joyous day of caribou hunting. The second, more typical of the older *pisiit* in Nunavut, is also about hunting but incorporates a number of circumlocutions that are characteristic of the genre. Indirect references are a mark of respect for the beings so identified. In song #8, even the composer's wife is referred to indirectly, as "my house's person." You will also see mention of "big black" (probably a musk ox) and the "big antlered one" (caribou). The composer begins the song with a modest statement about how hard it is to make a song. The "ptarmigan" reference may be another indication of modesty, in that references to small birds or animals are sometimes substituted in song texts for larger species such as seals or caribou.

ACTIVITY 2.2 *Listen to song #8 on the Tuhaalruuqtut site again, noting the way the diphthong* "a-i" *in the refrain is placed rhythmically and how this contributes to the gentle swing of the melody. Find other circumlocutions in the song text translations on this website.*

Many *pisiit* (see, for example, the text of page 9 on the Tuhaalruuqtut site) name specific places, sometimes in a series that traces the composer's travels over the land. To an outsider, these lists of place names may seem rather like a geography lesson. But to those who know the land in detail, memories of those places are evoked as each name is sung. In Inuit culture, drum dance songs map the land so specifically that they have been of use in "land occupancy" studies (e.g., the *Inuit Land Use and Occupancy Project*, 1976).

In a number of other Native American traditions, places are similarly evoked in songs, stories, and conversation. When investigating Apache concepts of landscape in the Southwest, for instance, anthropologist Keith Basso was taught that "wisdom sits in places." Apache Dudley Patterson used that phrase to indicate that one must remember everything about a place, its name, and events that happened there. He advised Basso, "Then you will see danger before it happens. You will walk a long way and live a long time" (1996, 70).

The words of Inuit elders reflect more than the facts of land use and echo the spirit of Patterson's words. As Anilnik Paniluk of Broughton Island said, "All peoples feel that their lands have a richness and life that go far beyond themselves. No person's sense of himself has to do only with the present, nor with only his own people. His lands have been occupied by other generations, other peoples, and their marks are, in a way, some part of his own mark on the land" (*Inuit Land Use and Occupancy Project*, 1976, 1:186).

Drum dance songs reveal much about the personality of the composer and his or her social relationships in the community. We already noted the assertions of modesty in one song. Singers who start their song with "Perhaps I will forget" or say that an animal is "impossible to catch" are often the ones who are known to have good memories or to be powerful hunters.

The themes of the songs referenced so far are comparable to others I collected and transcribed in an earlier book (Cavanagh 1982). To enable those who wish to investigate these song texts further, I include in parentheses the song numbers from that 1982 anthology.

A *pisiq* often expresses very strong emotions. Among the songs shared with me by people in the community of Kuugaaruq (Pelly Bay), one speaks of extreme loneliness; it was made by a man who was exiled from his community because he had committed a crime (70). Another was made by an elderly hunter who fears that he can no longer provide food for his family, although, in this case, one should remember the ironic circumlocutions and modest statements of some song texts and suspect that the individual may actually still be a very good hunter. Several composers sing about their shyness in performing at the drum dance (61, 75, 86), when in reality they were known as confident and fine performers. The *pisiit* of women (76, 81, and 58, for example) often relate to their children, expressing love and also concern about their well-being. One was made by a grandmother about her grandson who lived with her when they moved into their new Western-style house; another was made up by another mother to help her sons. One woman sings of her misery in having been separated from her own family when she married and moved to the community of her husband. Sexual exploits may be a narrative topic (72, 95). Drum songs may also communicate happy relationships, for instance with your *avvaq* (94), a person who shares your name.

ACTIVITY 2.3 *Browse the Tuhaalruuqtut Ancestral Sounds website for other songs that express similar themes. In addition, note texts that reflect experiences not discussed above.*

New experiences might be recounted in the drum dance tradition. In one case, a composer made a song to describe the first time he encountered an airplane, in 1955, a rare sight in that region in that decade.

Because drum dance songs express such emotional intensity in a public space, it is perhaps not surprising that some were used to settle disputes. A song could counter gossip about oneself or a member of one's family (48, 60, 92). In some cases, the resolution of a dispute seems to have been more formalized, with songs from each side presented one after the other.

Such an event was staged in the award-winning feature film *Atanarjuat*, directed by the acclaimed Inuit director Zacharie Kunuk with his colleague Norman Cohn, and produced by Isuma Productions in Iglulik. A rivalry between the title character and Uqi, both of whom love the same woman, is played out in one scene in the dance house. Their drum dances insult one another; each singer-drummer is accompanied by a *pisiq*, performed by his own team of loyal family members. Uqi's family sings,"When there is heavy meat to carry, he runs fast the other way"; right after that, Atanarjuat's family ridicules Uqi by suggesting that Uqi blames everyone else for his own failures. This is followed by a series of tests of strength. You can rent this DVD at most video stores in Canada and the United States.

The performance style of the solo drum dance arguably enhances the emotional intensity of the texts. The drummer often moves with his back to the singers and listeners. His drumbeat seems at first never to coincide with the song beat. Hence, he is rhythmically and arguably socially alone, without the coordination of the pulse that would enable him to feel at one with the singers. This tension between the song and drum pulses, however, bears careful scrutiny. Sometimes his drumbeat does coincide with the singing, and, as it turns out, this coincidence is patterned, occurring most often at the return to the *"ajaja"* refrain in each strophe. This is the point of relaxation or release in each stanza. Hence, the drummer is in his own world, but then brought back into the social space as the refrain returns.

In more recent staged performances of drum dancing, the drumbeats are frequently synchronized with the song beats. This represents a fundamental change in both the aesthetic and the social relationships of the performers. The tension between the independent tempos of the solo drummer and the chorus of singers has given way to a coordinated rhythm in all parts. The experience of drumming asynchronously but occasionally being brought back into the community rhythm feels very different from the experience of rhythmic coordination throughout.

As mentioned earlier in this chapter, this solo drum dance style is quite unlike the group dances of Alaska and the western Canadian Arctic. In the latter, a thin-framed drum is struck by a long slender wand that spans the entire diameter of the drum with each stroke. A group of seated drummers accompanies several dancers, who don't drum, unlike the solo tradition of Nunavut. The dances are often mimetic, imitating birds or animals, paddling, or even, in one recent song, playing basketball.

It has often been asserted that drumming was associated with shamanism, but there has not been much precise information available until the publication of a series of recent studies by the Nunavut Arctic College. See in Particular *Cosmology and Shamanism*. Most of these studies are available online at http://nac.nu.ca.

ACTIVITY 2.4   *Browse this website and make notes about what you learn about Inuit shamanism. Indicate where there are references to music in relationship to shamanistic practices.*

The elders who have chosen to share their knowledge indicate that only in certain locations and contexts was singing or drumming part of shamanistic practice. It is neither appropriate nor possible to consider this complex topic further in an introductory cross-cultural course on "Global Music."

INUIT MUSIC AS PLAY

ACTIVITY 2.5   *Write a think piece about the way the climate and residential space you live in influence your musical practices. Do you use your voice mostly indoors or outdoors? Do you use your ears mostly indoors or outdoors? Do you have sufficient privacy to be able to be loud when you want to be? Do you share music or enjoy it on your own? Do you listen to or make music differently in different parts of the space in which you live?*

People have observed that, in the Arctic, the outdoor spaces are vast but the indoor spaces are quite small. Household members live in close proximity, originally to maintain a comfortable temperature in a snow house or iglu, now perhaps to cut the cost of heating a bungalow-style home, perhaps because some Inuit enjoy togetherness more than privacy, or, in many cases, because houses are in short supply, causing unwelcome crowding. The original wood-frame homes built by the Canadian government when people were relocated into settlements in the 1960s were sometimes referred to as "matchboxes," since they were very small wooden structures without insulation. They were heated with a tiny kerosene stove and had very little furniture—perhaps a small table in the kitchen with a chair or two, and perhaps a mattress on the floor. The standard of living in northern communities has improved but still often lags behind other regions in Canada.

While drum dance songs enable people to remember the vast land, to recall specific places and the events and emotions that give meaning to those places, other repertoires are associated with indoor spaces. Women and children in particular have created games that bring joy and laughter to those spaces. Widely known across the whole of Arctic Canada and Alaska are juggling games in which the changing meters of the song counterpoint the steady rhythm of juggling three or more balls.

What is meant by "counterpoint" in this context? The rhythm of juggling must be consistent. The action of tossing and catching each ball creates a 1–2 pattern, but the word rhythms create a more complex cross rhythm. The recorded extract (CD track 4), for instance, begins with the following words: "*qulukpa qulukqulukpa* (3 + 5 syllables) / *usi suva nillipangunga* (2 + 2 + 5) / *aullatisama* (5) / *augigamik* (4) / *upingraganitut* (6) / *iqalik* (3) / *tutialigamisama* (8)." The syllable groupings constantly shift. While the jugglers would not think of these different word groupings as changing "meters," this European concept that indicates the organization of pulsation is related. One might describe the song as "heterometric" ("with varied meters"). Karin Kettler explained a juggling variation that makes the game still more challenging: "Some women don't catch the ball after it's been tossed. They let it land on their second hand so that the same hand that tossed it could catch it. This increases the difficulty." To both sing the changing patterns and juggle in a consistent duple pattern at the same time is a challenging task, and many times, the balls are dropped before the song has ended.

ACTIVITY 2.6 *Listen to CD track 4 while tossing a small ball or other object from one hand to the other. (If you are really good, try juggling two, three, or four balls.) Note that the tossing motion has a 1–2 rhythm. Shift your attention to the song. Try tapping your foot at the beginning of each word grouping using the text transcription above. The real challenge is to feel the two stress patterns simultaneously.*

While juggling songs may vary somewhat from one community to another, common bits of text and melodic/rhythmic motives are shared. One singer explained to me that these songs have "bits of this and that" in them. The recording you just heard translates as follows: "Ah yes. That one. I was cold. I was going out. Blood. In spring. A fish." Compare a (partial) transcription and translation (Figure 2.4) of a juggling song that is different but more complete than the extract on CD track 4. Some images ("blood," "fish") are common to the recorded song and the transcribed one below. Some phrases (the vocables *"qulukpa"* or lines 1–3 below) are untranslatable. Some lines refer to stories or legends. Some segments use indirect references that resemble drum dance narratives; line 5 below, for instance, describes "something that floats." Still others are scatological, referring to "snot" from the nose, or "shit" (lines 9 and 12). There is often no narrative connection between one phrase or image and the next.

Translation of the Beginning of the Juggling Song Text in Figure 2.4:

1. *Qulukpa qulukquluk pa* (not lexically meaningful)
2. *Tunit tunit tunit* (may refer to the Dorset Eskimos)
3. *Ajija*
4. Those boots,
5. They are something that floats (i.e., their seams are very waterproof)
6. Blood.
7. A slapping sound.
8. My aunt,
9. The hair on her forehead smells like shit.
10. The mouth of the bay.

11. My aunt and I are sharing.

12. We do not have a runny nose together.

13. The gravy,

14. I drank it all.

[Segment with names of persons]

FIGURE 2.4 *Musical transcription of juggling song excerpt.*

There are other game songs, for instance for hide and seek, and for competitive games. Even some string games, often called "cat's cradle," had songs associated with them.

In the communities of Nunavik and Nunavut, the games that have undoubtedly received the most attention both locally and internationally are women's vocal games, usually referred to in English as "throat singing." Nunavik Inuit call the game *katajjaq* (pl. *katajjait*), a word that does not seem to be translatable. The names in Nunavut are different. In Baffin Island, they are often called *pirkusirtuk*, and in Gjoa Haven and Kuugaaruq, games are named individually, although the name *nipaquhiit* (meaning "customary sounds") is sometimes used generically.

Jean-Jacques Nattiez has described vocal games as "a kind of 'host-structure' susceptible to absorbing sound sources of various origins: meaningless syllables and archaic words, names of ancestors or of old people, animal names, toponyms, words designating something present at the time of the performance, animal cries, natural noises, and tunes borrowed from petting songs, drum-dance songs, or from religious hymns" (1983, 460). In this regard, they resemble juggling song texts. One contemporary game plays with the three vowels of the Inuktitut language, A–I–U, but Karin Kettler observes that the order of the vowels differs from one region to another.

The vocal games migrated across the north by the end of the twentieth century and so regional distinctions are less apparent than they once were. Some differences among regional styles are still generally accurate, however.

Nunavut vocal games tend to be breathier, and several of them have lengthy texts that resemble the unexpected juxtapositions of images in juggling game texts. Each partner performs alternate syllables in the throat song "*Qiarvaaq*" (full name is "*Qiarvaaqtuq*"; CD track 5). This way of delivering a text, with the two partners alternating syllables, has been adapted to new types of music as well. Another vocal game uses the tune of an Anglican hymn. In addition to alternating text syllables, each partner sings alternate notes of the melody.

Nunavik games (CD track 6) use deeper throaty sounds and most use vocables. Certain communities are especially well known for their throat singers. Inuit advisors emphasized that this textbook should take care to "respect that this story or throat song is from that [specific] region or community." Puvirnituq, for instance, has been one important center for this art. Puvirnituq elders Lucy Amarualik and Alacie Tullaugaq (Figure 2.5) were among the earliest recording artists.

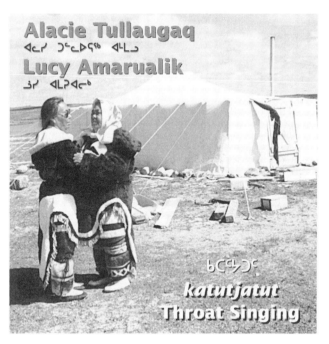

FIGURE 2.5 *Lucy Amarualik and Alacie Tullaugaq, shown on the cover of one of their recordings.* (Inukshuk Productions. Used with the permission of Inukshuk Productions.)

ACTIVITY 2.7 *Listen to* "Qimmirualapik" *(CD track 6), first focusing on the vowel sounds the throat singers produce, and then on the rhythm of their breathing, noting both inhalation and exhalation. Now listen for changes in the patterns from one section to another.*

Two women face each other at close proximity, often grasping the forearms of their partner and rocking with the rhythm of the game (see Figure 2.5). Kettler explains from a performer's perspective that "this helps the throat singers feel the rhythm and hear each other well when making changes (called *sanguagusiit*) in the sounds. Some throat singers stand inches from each other's faces." In some regions, they put their parka hoods up so that they can hear each other better. In some areas, a resonator is used—a large metal bucket, for instance, or a bread pan (see Figure 2.6).

They perform a series of short motifs in a tight canon: one woman imitates her partner one "beat" (or about half a second) later. The motifs include both breathy (unvoiced) and throaty (voiced) sounds, audible rhythmicized intakes of breath, pitched and non-pitched sounds. After a short while, the lead singer changes the pattern and her partner must follow. One throat singer says she can continue for as long as seven minutes, but often the song ends much earlier than that because the

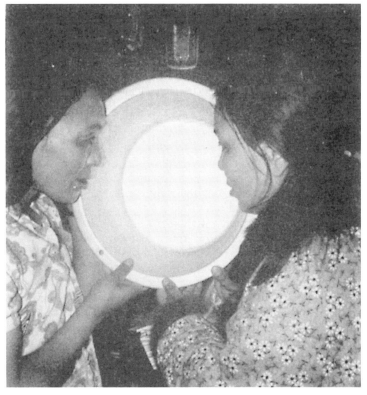

FIGURE 2.6 *Rose Kigeak and Kate Kamimalik from Gjoa Haven throat singing with a bread pan resonator.* *(Photo by B. Diamond, 1973)*

performers laugh, get out of breath, or feel light-headed from the rapid intake of oxygen. In some areas the games are competitive to see who can continue the longest. Karin adds that "what makes a good throat singer is someone who can last a long time, make a variety of sounds, and pick up the tempo."

Women often have special partners with whom they prefer to perform the games. Karin Kettler describes the importance of having a close relationship with your partner and also a voice that matches hers (CD track 7). She performs with her sister, Kathy, as "Nukariik" (meaning "two sisters") and feels their partnership is good both because their voices are well matched and they know each other so well (Figure 2.7). Their advanced skill level is also well matched.

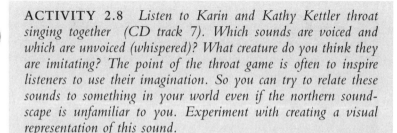

ACTIVITY 2.8 *Listen to Karin and Kathy Kettler throat singing together (CD track 7). Which sounds are voiced and which are unvoiced (whispered)? What creature do you think they are imitating? The point of the throat game is often to inspire listeners to use their imagination. So you can try to relate these sounds to something in your world even if the northern sound-scape is unfamiliar to you. Experiment with creating a visual representation of this sound.*

Most often the games imitate the soundscape of northern life: a puppy, polishing sled runners, the river, the wind, a mosquito. The throat song you just heard mimicked a *naujaq*, a seagull. When asked to try to create a visual representation, my students have often devised very creative ways to "transcribe" this throat song. One Native American student sewed a beadwork image of a bird flying behind a cloud. This challenges conventional Western ideas of what a transcription of music is, since it draws our attention to the source of the sound in a way that is consistent with ideas about the close observation of the environment discussed in Chapter 1.

Most ethnomusicologists have approached the issue of transcription from a very different perspective, focusing on the rhythms, text syllables, inhalation/exhalation patterns, and contrasts between voiced and voiceless sounds. Hence, their visual representations allow us to see a good deal about the production techniques but tell us very little about the timbre or shape of the gestures. Nicole Beaudry and Claude Charron (1978) creatively adapted a five-line staff notation (Figure 2.8).

FIGURE 2.7   *Karin and Kathy Kettler as Nukariit.*   *(Photo courtesy of Karin and Kathy Kettler)*

Digital audio software provides further tools for representing the timbre or quality of the vocal sound. A software program called Praat can produce a spectrograph of a small portion of the same throat song (Figure 2.9). Unlike the drawing of a seagull, or the adaptation of Western notation, this visual representation allows us to see how well matched the two voices are, and what exactly the pitch contour of the seagull cry looks like. We can observe the difference between pitched voiced gestures with clearly delineated bands of overtones and the noiselike throaty drone that underpins the bird cries. But the spectograph contains so much information that it is difficult to read.

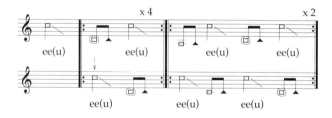

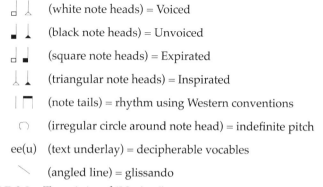

☐ △ (white note heads) = Voiced

■ ▲ (black note heads) = Unvoiced

☐ ■ (square note heads) = Expirated

△ ▲ (triangular note heads) = Inspirated

| ⌐ (note tails) = rhythm using Western conventions

◠ (irregular circle around note head) = indefinite pitch

ee(u) (text underlay) = decipherable vocables

＼ (angled line) = glissando

FIGURE 2.8 *Transcription of* "Naujaq." *(By B. Diamond after Beaudry and Charron)*

ACTIVITY 2.9 *The differences among the transcriptions in Figures 2.8 and 2.9 raise some important questions. Write a short essay that addresses the following questions: To what does each visual representation draw your attention? What does each transcription assume that you already know? Some limitations of the different transcription modes were mentioned above. Can you think of other limitations? Do we need a visual representation of any oral tradition? If so, why?*

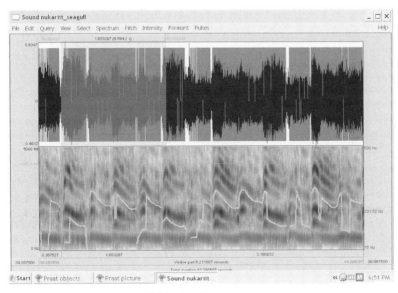

FIGURE 2.9   *Spectograph of* "Naujaq." *(Praat 4.4.13)*

NEW THROAT SINGING ENCOUNTERS: LOCAL-GLOBAL TENSIONS

When over sixty throat singers met at the first Throat Singing Gathering in 2001 to discuss their art, they shared their concerns about the appropriation of throat singing and they reminded one another that the meanings of specific games differed from one community to another. A widely known game concerning a small puppy, *"Qimmirualapik"* (CD track 6), was a case in point. Karin Kettler emphasizes that stories about individual games such as this one are also regionally specific. In one story, a little puppy hid in the entrance of the iglu and the women in the house imitated its hunger cries. In another version, a little girl wanted the runt of a litter to be the leader of the dogsled pack; she made him this throat song so that he would grow to be strong.

New audiences for throat singing and the attention of ethnomusicologists may be factors that have led to the wider circulation of local meanings and have influenced the popularity of certain games. It seems, however, that the most exotic-sounding games have often acquired a new currency for cross-cultural audiences. In a recent interview with Taqralik Partridge, the communication officer of the Avataq Cultural

Institute in Montreal, I asked how she would explain the popularity of *"Qimmirualapik"* and she said, "It's the weirdest one that people [non-Inuit] can hear. The best way to describe it sounds like you're making the sound of a motorboat. And you can't believe that women, especially women with high voices, can make that sound. It's the most mind-baffling" (personal communication, 2005). This game was the one that most startled and delighted collectors in the 1970s, including myself. As Partridge observed, the sounds challenged conventional notions of what a woman's voice could possibly sound like, and perhaps even what a human voice could sound like.

Perhaps for similar reasons, throat singing now attracts the attention of musicians the world over and is being widely revived in northern schools. It has become one of those genres that has a ready niche at international indigenous festivals. It has been enhanced by the incorporation of other media and musical styles. The duo Tudjaat, for instance, adds modern dance, pop music, and theatrical elements, and the two make videos for some songs.

The rock artist Lucie Idlout (Figure 2.10) incorporates her mother's voice and a sample of traditional throat singing in the title track of her debut album, *E5-770, My Mother's Name* (CD track 8). The title refers to a period of time when the Canadian government assigned numbers to regions (E5, for instance) and to individual Inuit (her mother was number 770). Lucie's anger over the dehumanization of Inuit through this system is contrasted with her own mother's rather joyous voice as a radio announcer in the 70s and then as a participant in throat singing both of which form an accompaniment to some sections of Lucie's complexly textured song.

The solo artist Tanya Tagak Gillis has recently collaborated both with Björk and with the Kronos Quartet to demonstrate how throat singing might be recontextualized in new ways. Her improvised performance in a song called "Ancestors" on Björk's 2004 album, *Medulla* (iMix #1), is described by her publicists as "a chaotic, elegant juxtaposition dancing pirouettes where angels wouldn't tread with hip-waders"(www. festival.bc.ca). As a soloist, she breaks from the tradition of a duet, and her vocal gestures draw upon but substantially change the traditional patterns. Not surprisingly, then, there are debates about authenticity in relation to this recent musical development.

Another new direction for throat singers is interindigenous collaboration. The timbral blend of *katajjait* with Tuvan "overtone" singing has become quite popular. One example, is a Canadian Broadcast Corporation recording made live at the 2005 Folk on the Rocks festival

FIGURE 2.10   *Lucie Idlout.*   *(Photo courtesy of Lucie Idlout)*

in Yellowknife, where the Quebec band Taima joined forces with throat singers from Taloyuak (Spence Bay), the Danish folk ensemble Instinkt, and the Tuvan group Chirgilchin.

It is interesting to contemplate why certain types of music, such as throat singing, have been globalized more readily than others, and what the implications are. Owing to the international interest of concert organizers, film producers, academics, and others, Inuit women have become increasingly worried about the appropriations of these vocal games. They are concerned both about changes in the traditional art and about intellectual property. One issue is that some performers don't know how to do the transitions between patterns, the *sanguagusiit*. Another is their concern about ownership. Some "composers" are known, but for the most part, the games are felt to belong to the women of Nunavik and Nunavut. An informal Inuit throat singers association, formed in 2001, has resolved to address these issues. They are considering the creation of protocols about the use of throat songs, or the possibility of group copyright to protect the throat singers from exploitation. Their struggle to control this form of "traditional intellectual knowledge" continues.

A vital part of Inuit modernity, staged performance and recording studio practices have had other, arguably subtler, impacts on throat singing. Acoustic resonators such as the bread pan, depicted in Figure 2.6, presumed one thing about the audience, namely that there was none. The singers performed *behind* the pan (or the bucket or cooking pot), not in front; similarly, parka hoods were isolating devices that created a listening experience that only the two participating women could properly hear. Onstage, however, performers increasingly play to their audiences. Some hold microphones, giving that close-miked, intimate sound but paradoxically preventing them from holding one another to feel the rhythm of the game. A physical intimacy has now given way to a sonic intimacy. Others use lapel mics so that they can continue to grasp one another's arms. In the recording studio, other changes may take place. Many producers cut out the laughter that ends live throat singing, for instance. And sometimes the balance between voices or the quality of the sound is changed.

In some ways, however, the studio production of Inuit throat singing stands apart from some of the mixing stereotypes that have emerged for many other Native American genres. For example, mixers use reverberation sparingly in throat song recordings. This may reflect the fact that throat singing has often been related to the extended vocal techniques of contemporary classical music. In the 1960s, composers such as Luciano Berio and Peter Maxwell Davies began to use a wide range of vocal sounds—whispers, squeals, grunts, moans, and speech, for example—in their compositions. Audiences who enjoy these "classical" compositions are often attracted to the diverse sounds of throat singing.

The style of audio production may also relate to the strong and distinctive sounds themselves, sounds that are surprising and hence attention grabbing. Such sounds are not easily exploited in New Age music. Surprises are inconsistent with the heavily reverberant wash of sound that characterizes the New Age production values applied to some types of Native American music.

These questions of generic associations are important since they shape the expectations of listeners. The expectations of listeners, in turn, contribute to decisions about which kinds of music remain local and which ones will be chosen to circulate transnationally. In the case of Inuit music, there is a big difference between the globalized genre of throat singing and other genres (drum dance songs, for instance) that have had less cross-cultural commercial attention. In such ways, then, recorded Inuit music is always implicated by processes of encounter, both within and among communities and cultures.

CHAPTER 3

Music and Historical Encounter: The Wabenaki and Other Eastern Algonquian Nations

1794—A flotilla of British ships arrive in Chebucto Bay. They will establish a settlement on land the Mi'kmaq had been using for hundreds of years. The Mi'kmaq are heard to comment, "There goes the neighbourhood."

(Mikmaq Book of Days online at http://mrc.uccb.ns.ca/calendar.html,
accessed January 7, 2006)

The eastern seaboard of North America is a region where First Peoples encountered Europeans at the earliest stages of exploration and colonization. The first encounters were with transient fishermen from various nations. Settlers and fur traders were not far behind. Initially, Native Americans were generous in helping the newcomers survive and in enabling them to find resources, such as furs, that they sought. The coureurs de bois of the northern fur trade companies, for instance, were undoubtedly First People or Métis who knew the waterways and the rugged wooded terrain. Native North Americans were integral partners in the emerging economies of the New World.

This was an area where Récollet, Jesuit, and Ursuline missionaries arrived in the sixteenth century, intent on converting the local population. There were also Catholic priests unaffiliated with a specific order. While Native Americans were cautious about adopting Christian practices, many adapted elements of the missionaries' belief systems to their own values and ceremonies. There were, as Willard Hughes Rollings has pointed out, a wide variety of interactions, ranging from "traditionalist-Christian factionalism" to the simultaneous practice of Christianity and traditional religion either overtly or covertly, from conversion to partial conversion or pretended conversion, and also hybrid faiths (Rollings 2002, 123).

This is an area where the concept of discrete First Nations is, in itself, problematic. Older histories tend to draw rigid boundaries around each nation and often overemphasize the conflicts that arose between them from time to time. As many scholars have noted (see, e.g., Prins 1996), however, it is increasingly clear that there was extensive sharing of land and resources, intermarriage, and collaboration among First Nations in the Northeast. Historical sources that mention St. Lawrence Indians, for instance, may be referring to Beothuk, Mi'kmaq, Wolastoqiyik (Maliseet), Abenaki, Innu, Mohawk, or some combination of people from these nations. Intermarriage both among members of different First Nations and between indigenous people and Europeans was commonplace, as were economic and military alliances. The best-known alliance was the Wabenaki Confederacy, the "People of the Dawn"—Abenaki, Mi'kmaq, Peskotomuhkatiyik (Passamaquoddy), and Burnurwurbskek (Penobscot) nations—formed in the seventeenth century to enable trading networks and to establish a stronger front in dealings with colonizers. But informal associations were commonplace as well. As a result, in Atlantic Canada many families are a complex mixture of Beothuk, Mi'kmaq, and Innu, as well as French, Scottish, Irish, or English ancestry. Historian Charles Martijn (2003) says that as many as 80 percent of the Mi'kmaq people on the west coast of Newfoundland have Innu kin. Their experience and cultural traditions call into question the sharp and impermeable boundaries we draw around indigenous "tribes" or "nations."

This is also an area, however, where the relationships between Aboriginal hosts and colonizers became strained as the struggle for land intensified. All along the Atlantic coast, Native Americans were forced from their traditional land bases to areas further west in the United States, Indian Territory (an official designation prior to 1907, when Oklahoma achieved statehood) in Oklahoma, or reserves elsewhere, or to more centralized and easily administered communities in Atlantic Canada. These enforced removals of various First Nations from their homelands to make room for European settlers had severe and life-altering consequences.

The Cherokee Nation, in particular, fought the Indian Removal laws of the 1820s and 1830s and, at one point, achieved Supreme Court recognition as a sovereign nation. Nevertheless, in 1838 they were forcibly removed from their homes to begin their journey to Oklahoma (Indian Territory) on what has been called the Trail of Tears. Seminole, Creek, and Choctaw were similarly made to trek westward. Christian hymns, such as "One Drop of Blood" (iMix #2) helped sustain them.

Some estimate that between 25 and 50 percent of those who made this journey died en route. Cherokee families who hid in the mountains of the southern Appalachians to avoid removal now constitute the core of the Eastern Cherokee. While this is one of the most widely represented instances of removal, the practice was widespread, as we can understand if we realize that many major cities along that seaboard rest on unceded Indian land.

Even where people stayed in a region close to their traditional land base, in Maritime Canada, for instance, they were often resettled to "growth" areas—communities such as Eskasoni, Shubenacadie, and others (described in Richardson 1993). In some cases, Atlantic seaboard nations were dispersed. Such is the story of the Narragansett, Wampanoags, Mashpee, and Pequot of Connecticut and Massachusetts, and kin further inland, such as the Sokoki. Even their names seem unfamiliar, because they were dispersed as a people for a period of time. Some have struggled to regain tribal status since the late-twentieth century. In other cases, such as that of the Innu nation, the names used by colonizers (Montagnais and Naskapi) are more widely known than the one in their own language. Because Innu and Inuit live in close proximity, outsiders sometimes confuse or conflate the two very different groups.

In the early twenty-first century, there are still many issues that have not been resolved about the rights of the First Nations of New England and Atlantic Canada. The Mi'kmaq of Nova Scotia struggle to assert fishing and resource rights. Their brothers and sisters in Newfoundland work to gain recognition as First Nations. The Innu people have, with some success, contested the disruption of their traditional way of life by a low-flying aircraft training program of the North Atlantic Treaty Organization, but they too struggle with problems, including resettlement to communities located where traditional hunting practices can no longer be easily maintained.

In the context of these struggles, both past and present, as well as of the many pressures for change, it is important to ask what role music could possibly play in defining, sustaining, and developing cultures. There is considerable evidence to indicate that song traditions were crucial elements. The remainder of this chapter explores three different ways in which song and dance traditions were used for renewal, mediation, and survival. First, we will consider the maintenance of older traditions of singing. We will look at those cultural practices that were private (and therefore often invisible to colonizers), those that affirmed relationship to the land and effected regular renewal of the relationship to the gifts of the land, and those that were traditionally designed to balance internal and external social relationships. Not only have many of these traditions remained strong, they are an important component of Indian modernity.

We then turn to the strategic and powerful uses made of music learned from or imitating colonial culture: both indigenized Christian and secular musical practices. The focus of the final section of the chapter is on contemporary social dances and songs of the Wabenaki nations and the revitalization initiatives that have been undertaken in recent decades. This most recent form of community renewal through music, like the historical practices in the Wabenaki region, draws upon diverse styles and shared repertoires. Each of these three sections demonstrates a way of using traditional knowledge to mediate encounters and to create contemporary Indian modernity.

RETAINING PRECONTACT FORMS
OF TRADITIONAL KNOWLEDGE

Spaces Beyond Colonial Control.   One of the means by which traditional knowledge was maintained in spite of the extensive disruption effected by colonization was to find spaces that were beyond colonial control. These might be remote physical locations or psychic ones that were inaccessible to outsiders. The Innu people, for instance, maintain a hunting culture that relies on traditional knowledge and relatively private spiritual practices. They do this, in part, by defining their world in terms of the mission-dominated villages and the "country," the latter being the remote and rugged inland areas of Quebec and Labrador. As anthropologist Peter Armitage explains, traditional knowledge is essential in the latter space:

> …non-Christian elements of Innu religious ideology cannot be properly learned unless the Innu spend time in the country. This is because the religion, like any other, is in many respects a "practical" religion; where knowledge is acquired through years of practice, hunting and handling animals, showing respect for them, dreaming about them, analyzing dreams, observing and performing ritual actions such as scapulimancy (a form of divination) and *makushan* (a feast), learning and reciting myths and being with elders in a context which encourages them to share their knowledge. (1992, 66)

While most Innu are nominally Christians and sometimes use Christian images or music in the country context, their beliefs are rooted in pre-Christian practices. It is clear that the traditional dealings with "animal masters" and forest spirits, the use of the drum, and in earlier periods the Shaking Tent Ceremony were all easier to conduct away from missionary eyes. There is a gendered aspect to this, as well. As Leacock (1980) has demonstrated, the Jesuit missionaries encouraged women in the community to stay close to the mission, but the men traveled more widely to hunt and fish. This meant that men retained traditional cultural beliefs but women rapidly became adept at negotiating with outsiders.

Songs, dreams, and drumming are all integral to Innu hunting practices. In virtually all First Nations communities, dreams (and related phenomena such as visions that are beyond conscious control) are taken seriously as a form of knowledge, a means of contacting the spirit world or acquiring personal power. For the Innu, dreams (*puamuna*) may be a form of prophecy, sometimes revealing animals that will be hunted the next day, or sometimes predicting future events involving family or distant friends. One Innu hunter told me that he dreamed of three animals on the shore and got three caribou the next day. A Labrador woman told me that she had dreamed of seeing a man across a body of water. Later she met this man in real life and decided, because of the power of her dream, to marry him. Armitage reports other features of Innu dream interpretation shared by a thirty-five-year-old hunter from the Labrador community of Sheshatshit.

> Dreams, for him, provide clues as to future hunting success and failure in the past…Dreaming about women, in his view, is particularly auspicious as it indicates that he will soon kill many animals. However, dreaming about a woman who is angry at you is bad; this means you will have no success at hunting in the near future. Dreaming about a cheque is good because it means one will soon kill many "money animals," that is, furbearing animals. The arrival of an aircraft in the dream indicates that a visitor may soon arrive at the camp. (ibid. 90)

ACTIVITY 3.1 *Write an essay on the importance you attribute to dreams and what may have influenced you to think about dreams in the way that you do. Compare the interpretations in the past two paragraphs with the sorts of interpretations you have made of your own dreams. Are there similarities as well as differences?*

Dreams are the only source of songs known as *nikamuna* (singular, *nikamun),* and in some areas they are also the means by which a hunter has the authority to use the *teueikan*, a frame drum that is central to Innu cultural identity (Figures 3.1a and 3.1b). That drum is like a window

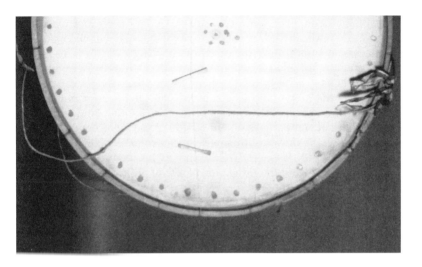

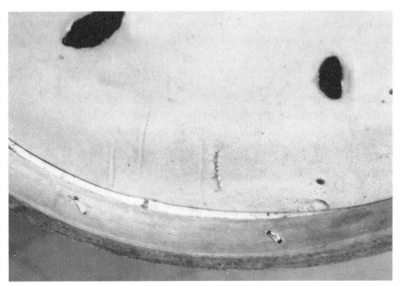

FIGURE 3.1   *a)* Teueikan *with red dots on membrane; b)* teueikan *with burned holes in membrane.*   *(Photos by B. Diamond)*

into the world of the dream. Hunters explain that they see animals on the membrane. One hunter told Armitage that "he sees 'sparks' on the skin of the drum. The size of these sparks, and their location on the drum head, indicate the number of caribou that may be killed and their approximate location in relation to the hunting camp" (ibid. 89). The story about sparks is particularly interesting because there are some drums that have holes burned in them. Many others have small red dots decorating the membrane. The color red and the ring of dots around the edge of a *teueikan* also symbolize the sun, another source of fire. A single snare at right angles on either side of the membrane is made of *babiche* (rawhide string) with small bones or wooden sticks; its sound is described as spirit voices. The drum may be kept unassembled until used. It is hung from the ridge pole of a tent, or, in a modern building, from a nail or hook on a rafter. While some think that its current form and aspects of its structure may have been influenced by the snare drums of the European military regiments, it is clearly an instrument that embodies beliefs about the spirit world and precontact religious practices.

When a hunter receives a *nikamun* in a dream, he may be able to reconnect with that dream when he later sings it to the accompaniment of the *teueikan*. This may be a relatively private performance, preceding the hunt. After a successful hunt, the drum may again be used for a *makushan* feast and dance. The marrow of the caribou tibia may be shared with fellow hunters, or community members may participate in a dance.

The drummer holds the bottom loop and, initially, strikes the skin in a rapid motion while speaking to the drum (Figure 3.2). His song may begin over this "tremolo" drumbeat, but the beat changes to a short-long pattern. Some say this change coincides with the moment when the drummer reconnects with his dream and sees the animals he will find by singing his dream song. This explanation relates to one interpretation of the dance. The slight dip to one side in the dancer's step is said to mimic an animal's gait, and the traditional alternation of men and women in the clockwise dance circle imitates hunters following caribou. In the dance, as well as in the dream interpretation cited above, women are associated with fur-bearing animals. The song is chanted within a small range, sometimes moving up or down microtonally. Most hunters insist that *nikamuna* are a private spiritual genre, not for the public domain. Hence, there is no audio example on the CD. In some communities, certain *nikamuna* are performed at festivals (see Figure 3.3).

FIGURE 3.2 *Thomas Noah (Cree-Innu) from Natuashish, Labrador, preparing to sing with the* teueikan. *(Photo by B. Diamond, 1981)*

Rituals of Renewal. As in most indigenous cultures, the gifts of the environment—the waters, the earth and the air—are honored in song and dance of the Atlantic coastal First Nations. Some events, such as the Green Corn Ceremonies (also called the "busk"), are major religious events for southeast tribes such as the Catawba, Cherokee, and Seminole. Local beliefs and practices differ, but the ceremony functions as a form of community renewal in each case. Giving thanks for the new corn crop is significant in that the crop ensures food for winter. But the occasion is much more than that, as Cherokee folklorist Rayna Green has explained: "[Green Corn] is a time of healing, forgiveness and of reconciliation. Before the Green Corn Dance, no-one can eat maize. Afterwards, maize is eaten to show how it is a symbol of continued life and good for the people" (1999, 76). Green notes, further, that several Creek, Seminole, and Choctaw sacred ceremonial grounds throughout the South are now threatened by development. "The tribes are struggling to hold onto them because of their significance in the life-renewal ceremonies of their people" (1999, 76).

The ceremony is a means of purification. Most enactments involve fasting and, in some regions, the drinking of a bitter black drink as an emetic. Levine, a scholar specializing in the Southeast, has helped me understand that many other kinds of purification, including scratching the arms and legs with needles or turkey quills, and abstinence from sex, may also be associated with Green Corn ceremonialism. Different communities variously incorporate stomp dancing, a stickball game, amnesty for past wrongdoings, and ceremonies to purify different foodstuffs (for more detail about Seminole and Creek traditions see Weisman 1999 or; regarding the mid-twentieth-century Cherokee see Speck 1951). It is possible that the Cherokee shared some aspects of Green Corn Ceremonies with the Haudenosaunee nations, since both groups once lived around the Great Lakes, before the Cherokee moved southeast.

Narratives and Performances that Relate to Encounter.   Well before the arrival of Europeans in North America, the Atlantic First Nations had developed various forms of traditional knowledge that seem to have been particularly well adapted to make sense of outsiders and foreign intrusions. Classic stories and myths, for instance, describe encounters with diverse creatures, human, spirit, and animal. The Innu culture hero Tshakapesh encounters a large-eared mastodon in one of his first adventures. The Mikmwesu of the Mi'kmaq, whose flute lures people far away, also evokes the idea of travelling far and possibly getting lost.

Traditional images have also been interpreted as teachings about encounter. As described in Chapter 1, the double-curve motif of the northern Algonquian nations is sometimes described as the mirroring of worlds: the physical and the spiritual, for instance, air and water, or natives and newcomers. Frank Speck was taught by Burnurwurbskek that the double curve was an image of peace (1940/1997, 160). Double curves adorned many handcrafted objects made by Mi'kmaq people historically. The peak hat associated with the Mi'kmaq women was often highly decorated, as were collars and borders. When new materials and European clothing designs were available, they were often adopted by First Nations people as an easier alternative to older styles of clothing, but traditional imagery was often retained. Contemporary designers continue to use this imagery.

Clothing in more remote hunting communities such as those of the Innu may also reflect beliefs about histories of travel and encounter.

Popular among Innu women since the nineteenth century are plaid skirts and blouses, with a shawl and Christian cross pendant, as well as a unique hat that has become a symbol of Innu identity. The red and black sectors of this hat, signifying sky and earth worlds, are held in place by a broad headband that is often beaded or embroidered. I was told that each row of beads represents another circle (a year, perhaps, or a stage of life) of a family's history. Although the hat may originally have been designed by a European, it was readily indigenized to become a mirror of the circle of life, a record of a family's journey and a trace of their encounters. Contemporary dance troupes (Figure 3.3) often choose to wear this style of traditional dress to symbolize Innu identity in staged performance.

The balance between internal and external affairs, even between peace and war, was often symbolically enacted in games. Furthermore, intercommunity conflict might be settled in a competitive game. Stick-ball games in which the object of one team was to hit the goalpost of their opponent with a ball propelled using a curved stick, or sometimes a net pouch, were popular in many eastern First Nations. Lacrosse is the form of this game that has become internationally recognized.

The ball game is highly ritualized among southeastern Woodlands peoples. Cherokee ethnomusicologist Marcia Herndon and anthropologist Raymond Fogelson have written about the role of music in mobilizing the transformative powers of this game. Herndon describes how, in

FIGURE 3.3 *Innu (Montagnais) dancers in traditional dress.* *(Photo by B. Diamond, 1987)*

the all-night dance that precedes the game itself, the men's songs bring strength to the players of one team as they take on the "red" power that will bring them victory. The songs that a male conjurer sings to accompany the women's dances, on the other hand, are associated with the color white, and their dance movements—linear, "back and forth in a restrained pattern and never from place to place" (1971, 343)—serve to weaken the opponents of the other team. The red-white dualism underlies social and political structures within their communities as well as without, and parallels a number of binaries—peace/war, passive/active, old/young, internal/external, plants/animals, cultivated/wild, female/male—that must be balanced in Eastern Cherokee society.

North of the Cherokee, among the nations of the Wabenaki Confederacy, games were less formal but probably also had traces of similar symbolism. While lacrosse was played, historically at least, the Dice Bowl Game, called *waltes* by the Mi'kmaq, is culturally more pervasive and significant (Figure 3.4). It is played with a flat wooden bowl and six bone or antler pieces with incised patterns. The dice are placed in the

FIGURE 3.4   *Mi'kmaq* waltes *game in progress.*   *(Photo by Franziska von Rosen. Used by permission.)*

bowl, which is used to throw them into the air and catch them again. Certain patterns yield certain counts. Each player has counting sticks and the game continues until one player has won all the counting sticks of the other. This is, then, like the stickball game of the Cherokee, a way of doing battle symbolically and peacefully. Stephen Augustine told me that when there were conflicts between communities, he thinks they were more often settled by a game of *waltes* between the community leaders than by warfare.

INDIGENOUS USES OF NEW PERFORMANCE TRADITIONS

Christian Hymns. The previous section focused on several sites in which traditional knowledge could flourish and on some of the ways in which it could function both to renew communities and to help them relate to the larger world around them. This section, on the other hand, explores the strategic adoption of the music of Euro-American colonizers. Two concepts will be addressed. The first is "syncretism," the theory that when there are similarities between two traditions, they are more likely to merge to form a new hybrid tradition. The similarities may be in the expressive forms themselves or in aspects of the social context for those forms. The second concept is "indigenization." It refers to a process by which new cultural ideas or expressive objects may be adopted but made or used as something that functions within the existing structures, institutions, or values of a society.

ACTIVITY 3.2 *Consider why it is useful to distinguish between these two concepts and write up your conclusions. Look back at the chapters you have studied thus far to see if you can find any other examples of either syncretism or indigenization.*

As mentioned above, Christianity was introduced to Native Americans as early as the sixteenth century. The conversion of Mi'kmaq Chief Membertou and his family in 1610 is often regarded as the point that marks the beginning of Wabenaki acceptance of Christianity. Stories about "Black Robes" or Jesuit priests are maintained in contemporary communities. Like the Wabenaki south of their region, the Innu of the St. Lawrence River and Lac St. Jean regions of present-day Quebec were undoubtedly served by the central Jesuit mission at Tadoussac at least as early as the beginning of the eighteenth century. Labrador Innu first encountered Roman Catholic priests much later and did not have resident missionaries in their communities until the mid-twentieth century. (On the other hand, as described in Chapter 2, the Inuit along the Labrador coast were not Catholic but were host to Moravian missionaries.) The Oblates of Mary Immaculate, who arrived first in 1844, became the order that had the most influence in Innu communities.

From First Nations perspectives, missionaries were often viewed as valuable symbols of political alliances or even as war councilors in the struggles between French and English, each with indigenous allies. Christian spiritual practices were often interpretable as similar to existing Native American practices. As Ann Morrison Spinney (2006) has explained in her study of religious syncretism among the Wabenaki, the Peskotomuhkatiyik of Maine viewed the role of the priest as parallel (and sometimes in conflict with) the role of the shaman, or *medeolinu-wok*. Both religious traditions used chanting and heightened speech for spiritual efficacy. Vocables such as "alleluia" were not unlike vocables in First Nations songs. Both traditions used chanting, prayer, and in some cases exorcism to treat the sick, and both had special repertoires for rites of passage such as the burial of the dead. These similarities perhaps made the Christian repertoires creditable and even powerful to the Native American parishioners. A syncretic blend of elements emerged, as Morrison has described very well for the Peskotomuhkatiyik of Maine:

> Music's role in facilitating this cultural encounter has been crucial. The stylistic affinities of the Catholic chant with indigenous ceremonial music allowed room for local interpretation, as shown in the burial hymns. Because Wabanaki congregations were without resident priests for much of the period after the French cession of Canada, they had to rely on traditional techniques of oral transmission to preserve their Catholic rites....In addition to stressing the syncretic nature of Wabanaki Catholicism, I have deliberately avoided focusing my discussion on Catholic practice as primarily political, cultural, or spiritual—one thing or another. That it can and has been all of these is the source of its efficacy for Wabanaki people. (2006, 76)

Of course, missionaries' responses to their indigenous parishioners were as varied as community members' responses were to them. From print documents, it is sometimes difficult to "read" the relationship. The letters the Jesuits sent to their superiors in France (known collectively as the *Jesuit Relations*), like documents of the Moravians along the Labrador coast that are referenced in Chapter 2, tell of many indigenous singers and instrumentalists who rapidly acquired European musical skills. The tone of these missives is often patronizing but invariably upbeat, since the letters were intended to impress the European colleagues and thereby contribute to fundraising initiatives for New World missions. Like contemporary media, their missives had "spin": they presented the missionaries in a positive light.

In other instances, missionaries got so interested in the culture of the First Nations that they neglected their job of conversion. Such is the case of Silas T. Rand among the Mi'kmaq. He allegedly failed to convert any Mi'kmaq, but his translations of many texts are invaluable, and his extensive collection of Mi'kmaq legends continues to be a significant and valued contribution.

A major part of missionary work was the translation of prayers and hymns into various Aboriginal languages. Of course this project relied extensively on the assistance of native speakers. The capability to print such books was not available until the early nineteenth century (see Figure 3.5), but handwritten anthologies of translated hymns undoubtedly existed earlier. The translations of hymn texts often substituted an Aboriginal concept for a Eurocentric Christian image. Karen Taborn (2005) has written of the Creek and Muskogee, for instance, that the Christian concept of "Savior" was translated as "one who is alive, one who breathes," and that Jesus might be translated as "chief." In some Innu translations of the Latin hymn "Veni Creator Spiritus," concepts that would be unfamiliar, such as "throne," are omitted, and the emphasis shifts to rejoicing and celebration. Contemporary First Nations Catholics assert that many new hymns were created by parishioners as well as clergy.

In some cases unique writing systems were adapted for publications. Among these is a system of Mi'kmaq pictographs (sometimes confusingly called "hieroglyphics") written on birch bark. While this system is thought to antedate the earliest Christian missionaries, it served missionary purposes as a means of teaching prayers and hymns to the new converts. Useful in a similar way was the system of syllabics developed by James Evans, a priest to the Cree, in the 1840s and adopted widely by the Cree and Inuit populations. Since both Cree and Inuktitut can be written with only three vowels, the direction of each syllabic character indicated the vowel and the shape of the character indicated the consonant that preceded it. Contemporary researchers suggest that the idea for the syllabic system may have been the markers (carefully broken tree branches and sticks placed in particular positions in or on the ground) that hunters leave to indicate their route to those who follow them. The Cherokee leader Sequoyah developed a notation for his language that was widely used in hymnbooks and other printed matter. For further information about these unique modes of writing music, see Levine (2002). In other cases, missionaries used European systems of music notation (Figure 3.5).

ACTIVITY 3.3 *Examine the two pages from Vetromile's* Indian Good Book, *3rd edition, of 1858 in Figure 3.5. What information is translated into Peskotomuhkatiyik and what is in a European language? What might this indicate about the use of the hymnbook?*

Print sources that reference only the titles of the tune rely on aural memory. The tune titles often refer to secular songs. We can deduce that these were known by the clergy and taught orally to their parishioners.

FIGURE 3.5 *From Emile Vetromile's* Indian Good Book, *3rd edition, 1858.*

The tunes, nevertheless, often had to be changed somewhat to fit indigenous word rhythms and vocal mannerisms. A favorite hymn, "Shuk tshi naskumitin," (CD track 9) among the Natuashish Innu (formerly from Davis Inlet) of Labrador illustrates this (Figure 3.6a). The performer, Mani Shan Nui, is one of the best hymn singers in her community, and for some hymns, such as this one, she uses an intense vocal sound in performance. The modal scale suggests a pre-seventeenth-century origin. A French cantique ("hymn"), "*Benisson a jamais,*" is referenced as the tune title in several mid-nineteenth-century

FIGURE 3.6A *Transcription of hymn performance by Mani Shan Nui of Natuashish, Labrador.*

hymnbooks, but the earliest music notation I have found (Figure 3.6b) dates from 1866.

THE TEXT FOR AN EXCERPT OF THIS INNU HYMN IS AS FOLLOWS:

Shuk tshi naskumitin.	Thank you.
Tapue espishiteian.	Let us really have faith.
Tshi ka shatshitiu.	He will care for us.
Tshe pimininiuana.	In that [other] life.
Tshi ka ininikituin.	You will live again.
Tshi minu ititin.	For you have done good things.
Mak tshi shigunumutin	When you shed
Tshin tshitshitua tshimiku.	Your Holy blood.

ACTIVITY 3.4 *Listen to CD track 9 and follow along with the text transcription. Note where the singer begins and ends. She does not regard the text as having the same fixed beginning and*

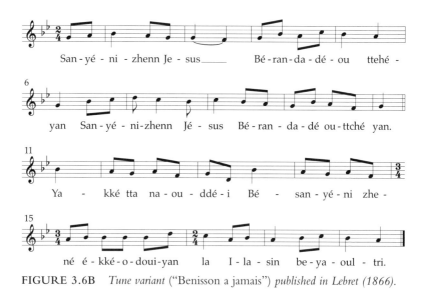

FIGURE 3.6B *Tune variant ("Benisson a jamais") published in Lebret (1866).*

end points as the print version. Note that the seventh degree of the six-tone scale is in between a natural and a sharp. Also listen to her vocal timbre. How might you describe it? Try to follow the music notation and note places where her performance diverges from the printed tune of 1866.

The tune in Figure 3.6b is clearly the same one that is currently used by Innu such as Mani Shan Nui. While in some cases the tunes have been modified over time, the fact that the same tunes indicated in mid-nineteenth-century sources are still in use today and still quite recognizable in relation to printed sources suggests that parts of the repertoire have been quite stable. There is some evidence that the least variable tunes were translations of Latin hymns for which we have music notation in Catholic sources such as the *Liber usualis*.

The performance spaces and uses of hymns were and are indigenized for a variety of reasons. In some cases, spiritual songs are needed for specific events of importance in the community. Wolastoqiyik elders in New Brunswick speak of a tradition of "noonday singing" in their communities, but we know little about this practice. In other instances, the place of performance dictates how both space and voice are used. Innu, for example, often take handwritten copies of hymns when they go into the "country," away from the village. Here a singer will turn toward the wall of the tent, the membrane that separates the outer world from the family inside, and use the hymn as a form of communication with that exterior world. Mani Shan Nui told me that "*Shuk tshi naskumitin*" was one of the "country" hymns. By analogy with the traditional hunter singing a *nikamun* into the membrane of the drum, the tent canvas becomes a surface through which (Christian) spirits might be summoned. Such hymns are described as forms of power, used to effect the right circumstances for safe travels, for instance. Their use, then, parallels that of the *nikamuna*, at least in the country context.

One of the most important Christian rituals for Wabenaki as well as Innu communities continues to be the celebration of Saint Anne, the mother of Mary. Many Innuat make an annual pilgrimage to the church of Sainte-Anne-de-Beaupré in Quebec City. For Mi'kmaq, Se't A'newimk (Saint Anne) is their patroness, and there are many localized stories about her. In some communities, she is said to be "a great helper and culture heroine who taught them moose-hair embroidery" (Howard 1962, 5). Combining the saint's festival with a summer council, many Mi'kmaq go to the chapel at Chapel Island, New Brunswick (Figure 3.7), a particularly important site, although there are many smaller ones as well. The week of celebration has several elements, including social dancing, meetings of political leaders about issues of concern, and often courtship. Saint Anne's Day attracts thousands of visitors on July 26 each year. Mildred Milliea, a Mi'kmaq from Big Cove, New Brunswick, who has written about Catholicism in her community, describes Saint Anne's Day as follows:

> The celebration of this event begins on July 26th, the feast day of St. Anne, and ends the following weekend with a picnic. The preparation would begin one week before all this is to take place. Men prepare the grounds around the church. They start by getting poles that would hold little flags for the procession path. A little ways from

FIGURE 3.7 *Saint Anne's Day procession at Chapel Island, New Brunswick, 1987.* *(Photo by Franziska von Rosen. Used by permission.)*

the church stands a big cross with a fence around it, and a gate that is opened for this occasion. The women gather and arrange fresh flowers and plants. Next a table is set up where the statue of St. Anne will be placed.

Everybody in the community would come for this feast day and the mass is sung in the same manner as Sundays, with the exception of certain hymns that are dedicated to the patron Saint. (For this occasion natives from other reserves would come and join in the celebration.) A special invocation hymn is sung (St. Anne Alasotmelseoin) during the procession to the cross. At this time the Chief, crucifix in hand, and usually four little girls with white dresses who have recently received first Holy Communion carry the statue of St. Anne. More prayers and singing are said and the Chief speaks to the congregation.

Once again another procession hymn is sung (Notaotiigemoet) as the procession returns to the church, and there again the elder will say the last prayer. It is only after all this solemn and prayerful celebration is over that the picnic would begin. The picnic lasts for three days and is filled with fun and laughter. Activities such as dancing, Bingo, games, and good times are enjoyed by all, including non natives from the surrounding area. (1989, 263–4)

Secular Repertoires and Contexts.   Outside of Christian church services, European music was heard and performed by First Nations musicians at social events both within and beyond the community. The historical record is, however, not always clear about the nature of collaboration. One unclear instance is a masque (a short theater piece with music) written in 1606 by Marc Lescarbot, a Parisian lawyer who came to Port Royal (now Annapolis Royal, Nova Scotia). Entitled *The Theatre of Neptune,* it is widely regarded as the earliest theater work in Canada. There are cues for a trumpet fanfare and a four-part song in the libretto, but the music has not survived. The libretto indicates that this was to be performed "upon the waves of the harbour"—presumably in canoes—in celebration of the return of two of the settlement's founders, Jean de Beincourt de Poutrincourt and Samuel de Champlain. There are roles for "*les sauvages,*" and some interpret this as indication that Mi'kmaq people participated in the theatrical production. Recent theater critics, however, draw attention to the racist labels for the roles and suggest that the parts may have been played by Frenchmen acting as Indians in a pattern of masquerade that would be replicated in nineteenth-century minstrel shows and still later in "cowboys and Indians" movies. Alan Filewod writes that the production was "a moment in which the theatre enacted an imagined authenticity even as it confirmed the extension of empire by transmuting the work of colonialism into spectacle" (2002: 34). Vigilance is always in order when interpreting the necessarily partial evidence of history.

By the late nineteenth- and early twentieth-century period, however, there are many examples of the way performance was used in response to colonization and racism, to negotiate and construct social relationships. As mentioned earlier, the Jesuits were intent on keeping women close to their missions, and thus women, in particular, played important roles as cultural mediators, often learning new languages along with Christian hymns and classical music. In the case of traditional hunting people such as the Innu, their men, on the other hand, continued to travel in the isolated, rugged interior of Labrador and northern Quebec in search of caribou or other fish and game.

By the late nineteenth century, Wabenaki women began to play intercultural roles. Stephen Augustine describes how Mi'kmaq women would take baskets and other crafts to urban markets because they could move in town with less risk of violence, relative to men. Sometimes they befriended African American railway staff members who would keep their earnings safe while in transit. This was also certainly true in the Southeast, where, for instance, intermarriage between Cherokee, Seminole, or Creek and African Americans was not uncommon. The growing body of biographical information available about such enterprising women indicates that they were often skilled performers, fortune-tellers, and businesspeople.

One such woman who mediated between cultures was a Beothuk named Santu Toney (b. ca. 1837) whose singing was recorded by the anthropologist Frank Speck in 1910, paradoxically almost a century after history books claim that the Beothuk were extinguished when Shanawdithit died in 1829. Santu Toney's grandmother was a white woman who was shipwrecked off the coast of Newfoundland and reared by Beothuk. Her father was a Beothuk who participated in the Red Ochre Ceremonies that are often said to have inspired the label "red" Indians. Santu moved in many different First Nations and nonindigenous social worlds. She first married a Mohawk, and later a Mi'kmaq chief. She traveled in New Brunswick, Nova Scotia, the Great Lakes region, and the northeastern United States living on money from basketmaking, beadworking, and fortune-telling. Hence, when she met Speck in Massachusetts in 1910, she was a cosmopolitan woman.

Her song (Figure 3.8; CD track 10) remains something of a mystery. Speck (1922, 66–67) tells us that the words were likely vocables, since

FIGURE 3.8 *Diamond and Hewson's transcription of Santu Toney's song, recorded by Frank Speck, 1910.*

she was "unable to explain because they had no sequence of meaning to her" and were "too inarticulate to be taken down." Linguists and anthropologists who have worked on the text subsequently have been unable to make a definitive text transcription or translation (Diamond and Hewson 2007).

ACTIVITY 3.5 *Photocopy the transcription in Figure 3.8. Listen to CD track 10 and note words that are particularly hard to decipher.*

Considering that she was so cosmopolitan, I think it is valid to expect that her "song" might in fact be several songs or song fragments. A number of ethnomusicologists have problematized the superimposition of the concept of a "piece" on all cultures' music. In Native American contexts, Francis Densmore was one who advised early collectors not to let a singer "run songs together" (cited in Gray 1988, ix). That seems to suggest that singers sometimes did "run songs together" (not knowing what was expected in the face of new recording devices), and I query whether that is exactly what Santu Toney did on this occasion. Several internal features suggest that three different styles are presented in this short performance.

What I labeled "part 1" of the song in Figure 3.8 seems to have a closed structure, since both the first and last two words and the melodic motives to which they are sung are mirror images of one another. The mirror relationship is coincidentally like the double curve described earlier in this chapter.

Text:	Word 1	Word 2 ... Word 2	Word 1
Musical motifs:	a	b b	a

The accents in Part 1 are irregular. If one can speak of meter here, it is certainly heterometric, unlike Parts 2 and 3. This part has six scale tones, corresponding to the notes A–C–D–E–F–G.

Part 2 is more chantlike, with few accents. This section bears a striking resemblance to some Innu hymns which have phrases that begin with an ascending leap and then unfold the text in a conjunct melody. The cadence patterns, moving from a second above or a third below the final note, are also like the modal Innu hymn tunes. We know that some of these hymns have been maintained in relatively consistent styles over several centuries, and it is possible that Beothuk learned some of these hymns, since intermarriage between the two groups was quite common. Part 3, on the other hand, has more regular accents in a triple meter, with cadences that imply a major key. It is the only part that has vocables and line repetitions (the final four text phrases are paired and the final two lines are the same). Many listeners think this part sounds "Western." Some hear lullaby-like features (perhaps the "do do do" vocables), while others associate it with children's songs such as "London Bridge." While these associations are clearly arbitrary and unreliable, it is not such a stretch to speculate that Santu Toney might indeed have heard such repertoires.

The stylistic contrasts may seem anomalous in relation to listeners' expectations. Do we expect that "Indian" songs are internally consistent? Further, if we allow that a logical expectation would be that each part emanates from a different repertoire source and possibly from a different source community, the performance makes a new kind of sense.

Santu Toney is perhaps one of the first indigenous singers to use audio recording not to represent a static culture but to bridge cultures. She may have tried to be conciliatory by acknowledging the music of people she associated with, or she may simply have felt that all these different styles were hers, as they undoubtedly were. The concept of recording one's voice, making it available to others, must have been a powerful experience at that time. It seems likely that the choice of what she sang in such a momentous circumstance would not have been arbitrary.

Like Santu Toney, a number of Burnurwurbskek women performers adapted to many different social worlds but still retained a strong sense of their indigeneity. Anthropologist Bunny McBride has written about the lives of several of them. Molly Spotted Elk and Lucy Nicolar were among those who created a unique style of "Indian vaudeville" in the early twentieth century.

The dancer and actress Molly Spotted Elk (1903–77) found sympathetic audiences especially in Europe, where she performed at times in a full feather (Plains) headdress—unlike any apparel of her own nation but undoubtedly a marker of "authenticity" for her audiences. Lucy Nicolar (1882–1969), a Burnurwurbskek from Old Town, Maine, performed as Princess Watawaso on the Chatauqua circuit, but also staged pageants in her own community, where she ran a craft business for many years. She rarely missed a chance to sway her audiences to consider her people's issues, the loss of land and human rights. McBride quotes an instance of this "artful activism" as described in the *Bangor Daily* (January 12, 1900)—an incident at the Women's Debating Society in New York City. Princess Watawaso attended a (very conservative) debate about whether immigration was dangerous and threatening to all true Americans. The Maine journalist whom McBride quotes writes as follows about the Princess:

> She arose to speak, her stately form commanding instant recognition … "I believe I am the only true American here. I think you have decided rightly. Of all my forefathers' country, from the St. John to the Connecticut, we have now but a little island one-half mile square. There are only about 500 of us now. We are very happy on our island, but we are poor. The railroad corporations, which did their share of robbing us of our land, are now begrudging us half-rate fare. But we forgive you all." There was a long silence, and the subject was laid on the table. The president said that the musical feature would have to be omitted as the pianist was sick, and "would someone please volunteer?" No one had the courage to try an impromptu before that large audience. At last who should beg to be allowed to try but Wah-Ta-Waso, who played some selections from Chopin with the greatest ease and sang a plaintive air which touched the hearts of all those present and made them feel like doing anything in the world for her. (2001, 141)

These examples reveal a remarkable capacity for moving between worlds, earning respect in mainstream circles without missing opportunities to present Native American social issues to a broader audience. Furthermore, the stories of women such as Santu, Molly, and Lucy imply that colonization and the development of Native American "modernity" was experienced differently by men and women.

CONTEMPORARY WABENAKI SOCIAL DANCE AND SONG TRADITIONS

The Wabenaki Confederacy, an alliance of First Nations in the Northeast including the Abenaki, Wolastoqiyik, Mi'kmaq, Peskotomuhkatiyik, and Burnurwurbskek, was formed in the seventeenth century for a variety of reasons. It facilitated the development of trading networks, ensuring the necessary collaboration of people in different regions and along different waterways. This created a measure of community stability (albeit in a period when colonial wars implicated Native Americans at every turn) and encouraged peaceful relationships among the First Nations involved. The allied nations hoped to present a solid front, both economically and militarily, when dealing with European colonizers. This hope was not always realized; some nations, such as the Abenaki, were buffeted between the French and the English from time to time. Fundamentally, however, the establishment of the Confederacy inaugurated a period of international relations. As with the Iroquois Confederacy, discussed in Chapter 4, these relationships were usually confirmed in wampum records. The purple and white shells of the quahog clam provided the material for the contrasting colored beads that were woven into patterns symbolizing the structures of alliance. As described in Chapter 1, the ceremonies enacted in conjunction with wampum exchange were an important part of the alliance process. They facilitated an exchange of cultural knowledge, including song and dance.

There were many reasons for Wabenaki people to meet. We have already seen how even Christian celebrations such as Saint Anne's Day were amalgams of religious observance, social celebration, courtship opportunities, and political meetings. Many different kinds of meetings were called "*mawiomi*," roughly translated as a "gathering." They might be gatherings related to trade, or to weddings that, in older times, often involved several couples and family from various communities who would gather when the priest was resident in the summer. Today a *mawiomi* might refer to a meeting of the Grand Council of the Mi'kmaq or to a powwow.

Chief-making ceremonies were particularly significant gatherings, validating and celebrating new leadership in the community. According to Leland and Prince's account of 1902 (see Smith 2004), people might travel as far as one hundred miles to attend such an event. Smith describes the Peskotomuhkatiyik songs performed at Indian Island, Old Town, Maine, in 1953:

> Songs were an important part of the entire occasion, including the formal part performed only by the men. The number of greeting songs depended on the number of visiting dignitaries and the number of inductees. State and provincial election laws made it no longer necessary for neighboring chiefs to be involved in the election process; in 1953, the songs for that part of the ceremony were remembered, but were not included in the ceremony... In 1953, the Passamaquoddy retained a Welcoming Song to the visitors who were there as spectators. An old woman in costume sang the Women's Greeting to the Chief and the Children's Greeting Song to the Chief. She danced toward the Chief when she sang and back to the troupe when the Chief responded with his Greeting Songs. [In 2003], only the Passamaquoddy have retained a semblance of this part of the performance, reducing it to a Greeting to the Chief and Lt. Governor from the women and

children, which was their acceptance of the new leaders. The songs
were virtually the same [as in 1953], changing only the names, titles
and roles of the visitors. (2004, 401)

Smith also describes a Burnurwurbskek Chief-Making Ceremony at
which there was a Snake Dance and a Pine Needle Dance as part of the
social events following the "solemn rituals" (2004, 402).

Many of these song genres continue to function as genres of social
music and dance in contemporary communities, although traces of
their ceremonial functions are still remembered. The Snake Dance is
a case in point. A Peskotomuhkatiyik Snake Dance song was shared
with Jesse Walter Fewkes, who made the earliest recordings of Native American music in 1890. We know, then, that this song tradition
has been maintained by Mi'kmaq and other Wabenaki for more than
a century. Recently, anthropologist Trudy Sable made a study of the
many layers of meaning this dance has for Mi'kmaq people in Nova
Scotia. She writes:

> In my own research into the legends, songs and dances of the Mi'kmaw
> people of eastern Canada, I have come to see how everything was a
> mirror of everything else. For instance, in researching the "Serpent
> Dance," the dance not only mirrored the exuviation of the snake, but
> was associated with a particularly powerful medicine, which was asso-
> ciated with the *jipijka'm* or horned serpent seen in numerous legends.
> The medicine mirrored the qualities of the *jipijka'm* and this was all
> mirrored in a constellation in the sky. Furthermore, the dance was part
> of the "turning over of seasons" that one sees in other legends. Stars, as
> seen in songs and legends, were where animals and birds came from,
> and the telling of any legend or singing of any song was a sharing of
> your life force. This is a very simplistic rendering of this research, but
> the point is that wherever one looked in the world, a person could see
> a reflection of where they were and a reminder of the interrelatedness
> of all the realms of existence. (1998)

In contemporary performance, the Snake Dance has a call-and-
response pattern, and this stylistic feature, along with the movement
of the singer-dancers through the community, bears resemblance to
some forms of the different stomp dances that are so prevalent among
both Haudenosaunee and southeastern nations. The "humba husha"
phrase (CD track 11), for instance, is the same as a pattern in the
"Unity Stomp," available in our iMix and brought up in Chapter 4.
The Mi'kmaq Snake Dance pattern is also similar to the intertribal
Snake Dance or Friendly Dance performed at some contemporary pow-

wows. Similar cognates among social dance songs have been traced in the Southeast (see, for example, Levine 1991, Jackson and Levine 2002). The Denny family (Figure 3.9) of Eskasoni, Nova Scotia, heard on CD track 11, have been important culture bearers in the maintenance of song repertoires.

ACTIVITY 3.6   *Listen to CD track 11, a Snake Dance performed by the Kitpu Singers whose members are the Denny family of Eskasoni, Nova Scotia. Learn some of the responses and sing them along with the recording in response to the leader's call.*

Many Wabenaki social song and dance repertoires point to relationships among communities. A repertoire of "trading songs" and "wedding songs," for instance, is known in some communities. The tradition of welcoming songs continues to be used when important political or social leaders visit Wabenaki communities. The Wabanoag Singers, a Wolastoqiyik group led by Margaret Paul, greeted Queen Elizabeth and Prince Philip with a welcoming song when they visited New Brunswick in 2002. Like Sarah Denny, Margaret Paul is another figure whose role in the revitalization of music and other traditional teachings has had a major community impact.

FIGURE 3.9   *Sarah Denny (center) with four of her daughters and Peter Googoo, 1986. Sarah and some of her daughters wear the traditional peaked hat described in Chapter 1.   (Photo courtesy of the SPINC Research Project. B. Diamond, director)*

Welcoming songs are also widely known by Newfoundland Mi'k-maq. *"I'ko"* (CD track 12) is one of them, even though it may have originated elsewhere; some Mi'kmaq and Wolastoqiyik describe this particular song as a gift from the Mohawk nation, their eastern neighbors (see Alstrup 2004). CD track 12 is a performance by Susan Hill from Conne River, Newfoundland; she was first taught the song in her school choir. Susan explains that the exchange of this song was a gesture of peace between the nations. (A variant of this same song, performed by the Wabanoag Singers, is available on an album entitled *Heartbeat: Voices of First Nations Women* (1995), legally downloadable at www.folkways.si.edu.

Another well-known welcoming song is called "Kwa'nu'te" in Mi'kmaq but is also known in Peskotomuhkatiyik, Burnurwurbskek, and Wolastoqiyik communities. This song inspired a film about Mi'kmaq artists in Nova Scotia, directed by Mi'kmaq filmmaker, Catherine Martin (see *Kwa'nu'te* in the Resources list). The late Sarah Denny performs the song in the film.

Many other social dance songs convey a mirroring of the environment. A very popular social dance song among contemporary Mi'kmaq is the dance *"Ko'jua,"* performed by Sarah Denny (CD track 13). She refers to the *Ko'jua* dance in conjunction with a "partridge song," in which the fast tempo and changing rhythmic groupings mimic the quick and unpredictable movements of the partridge. *Ko'jua* is sometimes used as a more general label for "Mi'kmaq dance song," however, and is also sometimes related to the Mi'kmaq style of "smoke dance" described in Chapter 4 (Janice Tulk, personal communication, 2007). Furthermore, there are several different songs labeled *"Ko'jua."* One by the group Eastern Eagle is in our iMix 3. Another, by the group Morning Star, is a contemporary composition referencing the traditional song and dance. The complex way that titles move across the repertoire, then, is evident in the case of the various *"Ko'jua"* songs and dances.

The qualities of natural materials such as pine needles also inspire social dance categories. The Pine Needle Dance is associated with women, and, in early twentieth-century accounts, it was performed playfully with pine tips (representing dancers) bounced on a board. Frank Speck described the game as follows:

> Anywhere from six to a dozen tips of white pine sprigs are trimmed squarely across the ends to represent dancers. They are stood pointing upward upon a slab of wood, then by jouncing and shaking this, a lifelike imitation of human dancing is produced. As the player

sways and jounces the board, she sings dance songs while the pine tips twirl, topple, slide, or circle around, sometimes in pairs jostling one another. They eventually fall, upsetting each other till all are down...The last "dancer" to remain on the board is praised for her skill and endurance, as the pine tips are supposed to be women. (1940/1998, 183).

At present the dance is done a bit differently. The pine tips are placed on the drum and when they vibrate and move around, the direction they go determines the direction that the dancers move (S.C. Francis, personal communication, 2006).

It is more difficult to determine how the songs have changed over time. There is evidence that tunes migrated and changed function from one community to another. A case in point is the "Pine Cone Dance Song" (CD track 14). The version on CD track 14 was recorded by the Spirit of the Dawn singers, a Burnurwurbskek group from Old Town, Maine. The same tune is transcribed by Frank Speck (Figure 3.10) in his book *Penobscot Man* (1940/1998, 280), where it is labeled a "round dance" or "wedding song." The Old Town Burnurwurbskek also perform a Rabbit Dance of the Haudenosaunee. Hence, the exchange among nations, and the renaming and multiplication of stories about song origins and meanings continues.

Wabenaki Cultural Revitalization. The ease with which songs are shared and used in new contexts has been important for the revitalization initiatives that have taken place in both the Northeast and the Southeast (see Levine 1993) since the 1980s. One part of this movement has been the "recovery" of drumming. It is not clear, however, how or even whether drums were used historically by the Mi'kmaq and Wolastoqiyik nations. For the northern nations—the Mi'kmaq in particular,— descriptions abound of song accompanied by striking a sheet of birch bark, sometimes placed over a hollowed-out space dug in the earth. A small wooden tray, struck by a wooden stick, is still sometimes used as a song accompaniment (Figure 3.11). A split ash stick called the *ji'kmaqn* is another sound producer used to accompany song (Figure 3.12).

Their Peskotomuhkatiyik and Burnurwurbskek neighbors to the south, on the other hand, maintain a drum tradition that dates at least to the early nineteenth century. And, as mentioned earlier, the Innu of Labrador and northern Quebec continue to use the *teueikan* as a hunting tool and spiritual aid. There is, however, very little clear evidence

FIGURE 3.10 *Round Dance transcription from Frank Speck's* Penobscot Man *with section that is melodically like a contemporary Pine Cone Dance song of the Spirit of the Dawn Singers.*

of drums in Mi'kmaq and Wolastoqiyik communities. Were they ever used? Were they simply lost for a time? Some believe that the missionaries destroyed drums and that their contemporary use is a reclaiming of a prior tradition.

A number of individuals were involved with bringing the drum and its associated traditions (back) to the Wabenaki nations. The Wolastoqiyik and Peskotomuhkatiyik women of St. Mary's, New Brunswick, sought out Ontario teachers and had a large, powwow-style drum made for their community. A leader among them was Margaret Paul, mentioned earlier. The Birch Creek Singers of Big Cove, New Brunswick, and their leader Tom Paul introduced the powwow drum to the Mi'kmaq. They in turn carried the big drum to the people of Conne River, Newfoundland. Today, a number of powwow drums are active, as described further in Chapter 6. Among the longest-standing groups is Free Spirit, many of whose members now participate in the group Eastern Eagle. The Indian Bay Singers are an important contributor to northeastern powwows. The leader of the Medicine Dream band, New-

FIGURE 3.11 *Tom Paul (Mi'kmaq) with wooden instrument he made based on historical descriptions.* *(Photo by Franziska von Rosen. Used by permission)*

foundland Mi'kmaq Paul Pike, is also deeply involved with powwow. His band uses the repertoire of the big drum, traditional Mi'kmaq songs, and contemporary songs, many by Pike himself, in their thoughtful arrangements.

The revitalization of traditional Mi'kmaq songs has similarly been due to the dedicated work of a small group of people. The Denny family of Eskasoni, Nova Scotia, whom you heard on CD track 11, played

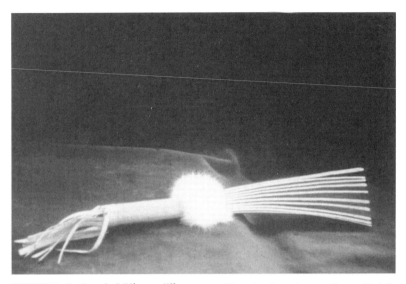

FIGURE 3.12 *A Mi'kmaq* ji'kmaqn. *(Photo by Franziska von Rosen. Used by permission.)*

a significant role in this revitalization. They made one of the earliest recordings, featuring elder Sarah Denny and the Kitpu drum, consisting of younger Denny family members. ("Drum" is a term that refers not only to the instrument but also to the players associated with it.)

Another important figure in the late twentieth-century cultural revitalization was Mi'kmaq George Paul from Metepenagiag (Red Bank), New Brunswick. He made a cassette recording of traditional songs that circulated widely in the 1980s. Mi'kmaq people throughout Atlantic Canada used it to learn songs. Some were traditional and others were newly composed by Paul himself. The cassette includes audio tracks with explanations of each song. The values that informed cultural revitalization are evident in the history of the Mi'kmaq honor song "*Kepmitétmnej,*" which George Paul composed. He describes his motivation as follows, on the recording he made:

> Hello, my name is George Paul. I am a Mi'kmaq Indian and what I am going to do for you is sing you some Mi'kmaq songs and chants. Some are recent and some are ancient. I will introduce the chants

and songs before I sing them. The first one is an honor song, the Mi'kmaq honor song. It is very important that every nation have an honor song. This one is directed towards the Mi'kmaq nation. (audio introduction, *Micmac Traditional Songs*, 1980)

It is interesting that he does not claim authorship of this song or tell us its source. But when ethnomusicologist Franziska von Rosen was doing research in his community she learned more about the origin of this song. She writes:

> Then one evening, as a group of us were sitting in Stephen Augustine's living room, on the reserve, George talked of how this song came to him during a fast in Alberta. He spoke of having been deeply saddened by the fact that the Micmac Nation did not have an honor song; that the spirits responded to his grief by giving him this song for the Micmac people. According to George the song was needed, it was asked for appropriately and it was given. Nobody in the room questioned its authenticity and the community had officially accepted it as their honor song. (1998, 241)

The mode of receiving a song is the important element here, as well as the acceptance of the influence of other places and other nations. Some listeners hear a relationship to hand game songs of Alberta Cree, while others hear Haudenosaunee influences in the style of this song. Contemporary Wabenaki culture, then, draws upon different sources and is an amalgam of local and intertribal elements. This Mi'kmaq honor song has been widely circulated and frequently recorded since the early 1990s by Free Spirit, the Denny family, the Sipu'ji'j Drummers and others (see Resources list). Stylistically, it does not resemble the social dances of the Mi'kmaq but rather has the melodic shape of powwow songs. The vocal style, however, as well as the language and sentiments of the text are clearly Mi'kmaq. Eastern Eagle's performance of George Paul's honor song is available on the iMix (#4) for this text.

As already implied, recordings have played an important role in revitalization. The locally circulated cassette of George Paul and the independently produced cassette of the Denny family, in particular, have been widely influential in Mi'kmaq communities. By their repeated performance on recordings, certain songs have been canonized, among them the Mi'kmaq honor song composed by Paul, the welcome song "*Kwa'nu'te*," and the social dance song "*Ko'jua*," discussed earlier.

Other Wabenaki musicians whose work extends into powwow, country, rock, and hip-hop, among other genres, have continued the long tradition of borrowing and adapting music to create hybrid styles. Some examples are discussed further in Chapter 5. The various strategies for negotiating with music—forming alliances, sharing, and welcoming, among them—that I have described in this chapter continue to contribute to the contemporary strength of the cultures.

CHAPTER 4

Music and Historical Encounter:
Haudenosaunee Music Culture
with Occasional References
to Cherokee Traditions

The Haudenosaunee have maintained a strong and continuous cultural presence in the agricultural heartlands of southern Ontario, Quebec, and New York State. Their language and traditions continue to be a central part of their modernity and a means by which outsiders are encouraged to share in the celebration of the gifts of the earth that sustain life. To get a sense of what the three themes of this book mean in the Haudenosaunee context, consider an ethnographic description of a contemporary event—one that embodies traditional knowledge, encounter, and modernity.

ATTENDING A "SING"

If you live in or near a Haudenosaunee community, you may have an opportunity twice a year to attend a "Sing" in one of the Longhouses that are, today, somewhat comparable in function to churches, synagogues, or mosques. (A "longhouse" was once a place of residence for several families who shared a central fire; it is also a metaphor for the Iroquois Confederacy, as discussed below. So the same word refers to different, but related, things.) Established in their current form in the 1960s, these gatherings feature performances by the "Singing Societies" of each community. Singing Societies exist to raise money to help those in need. Their members may buy groceries, or see that someone helps repair the roof on someone's house, or do a host of other charitable acts. All the funds they raise contribute to the well-being of members of their community.

A "sing" may bring together as many as five hundred people from New York State, Ontario, and Quebec, and so preparation begins early in order to ensure that everyone is fed and accommodated. There are a lot of potatoes to peel!

On Saturday afternoon, people begin to gather at the Longhouse and take seats in the rectangular, wood-frame building. An elder delivers the Ganǫhǫnyǫhk (Thanksgiving Address) to begin the proceedings. You already heard an excerpt of this speech, as spoken by Gordie Buck in the background of Santee Smith's composition (CD track 2). The words for a different performance, published by the Grand River Poly-technic in Brantford, translate as follows:

> *This gathered crowd all will listen to what has become a responsibility,*
> *That we pull these words that the Creator gave us*
> *For the giving of thanks.*
> *It is with great joy that we are thinking of peace and wellness.*
> *Therefore we will, as one, lay down our minds and greet each other.*
> *Let it be this way in our mind.*
>
> *Now we will tell all about the earth.*
> *That is where we rest our feet upon, our mother, we call her.*
> *That is where our Creator planted everything.*
> *She is still growing everything so we will*
> *Have wellness and peace in our thinking.*
> *Therefore it is with great joy that*
> *She is still doing what responsibilities he gave her.*
> *Therefore we will carefully give her thanks.*
> *The earth, our mother we call her.*
> *Let it be this way in our mind...*

The address continues, acknowledging the plants, fruits, trees, animals, waters, food for sustenance on earth, winds, sun, grandmother moon, stars, Handsome Lake, the four sky people, and the Creator. The elder is speaking, not singing, but the cadence of each section and the deliv-ery give it a certain songlike quality. The text varies with each speaker. There is no single cultural authority, no fixed "scripture," but rather individual interpretations of the gifts of each part of Creation. You can hear elder Jacob Thomas deliver a third version of the Thanksgiving Address online at www.tuscaroras.com.

Once the gifts of Creation have been acknowledged in the Thanksgiv-ing Address, the sing may continue. One group of singers after the other, perhaps as few as four or as many as twenty-four, take their places on the two parallel benches in the center of the room, half on one side, half facing them on the other bench. As Sadie Buck describes it, the voices meet and go up to the Creator. They begin to sing a series of Ęhsgá:nye: (var. *eskanye*) new Women's Shuffle Dances, the genre of social dance music that is actively composed today.

The lead singer plays a small water drum, made from a hollowed log or perhaps a piece of plastic pipe and carefully tuned by drawing the wet tanned skin tight with a cloth-wrapped ring (Figure 4.1). It has a clear pitch, much higher than either frame hand drums or the big pow-wow drum (described in Chapter 5). The water drum will be turned over periodically to keep the membrane wet, an action that slightly

FIGURE 4.1   *Hubert Buck Sr. playing the water drum.*   *(Photo by Sam Cronk. Used by permission.)*

lowers the pitch. It may be further adjusted by breathing into the drum through a small air hole on one side that has a spigot in it.

Drumsticks must feel well balanced. They may be simple or very elaborately carved. Occasionally, a drumstick will be carved with a small ball that moves (and clicks) inside the stick handle. The skill it takes to carve this intricate object from one piece of wood is truly admirable.

Each of the other members of the group chooses a cow-horn rattle from a bag where they keep a good supply of these shakers. Cow-horn rattles make a gentle but crisp sound, because they are filled with small, hard objects such as BBs. The cow-horn rattle players-singers will "prop up the song." There are many other Haudenosaunee shakers, but they are used for ceremonial rather than social events. The gourd shaker, chipmunk sticks made of hickory, and bark shaker are among them. The turtle-shell rattle (Figure 4.2), associated with both medicine "doings" and the Great Feather Dance of the Midwinter Ceremonies in the Longhouse, is the most elaborate of all. Made from the head, neck, and shell of a snapping turtle, the turtle-shell rattle is filled with pebbles or

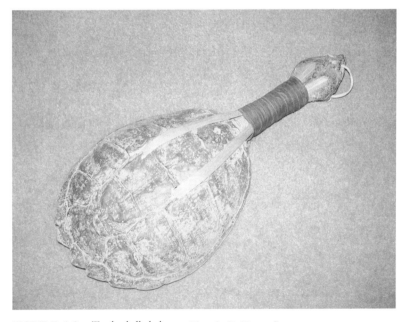

FIGURE 4.2 *Turtle-shell shaker.* *(Photo by B. Diamond)*

cherry pits as rattlers, the leg and tail openings are sewn closed, and the neck is extended with one or two hickory slats and wrapped with buckskin or hockey tape to form a handle. For the sing, however, only the water drum and cow-horn rattles will be used.

There are old Ẹhsgá:nye, some said to predate the arrival of Columbus, but today, most groups perform relatively new ones, grouped in sets sometimes described as "wheels." The audience is attentive, although much joking and chatting takes place in the interval between performances by different groups. The singing continues until it is time for dinner. But only for a short while. The "social"—the part of the sing that includes dancing—will start before long.

The evening social begins with the Standing Quiver Dance (*Gadā:tro:t*), a call-and-response stomp dance with no accompaniment. This type of stomp dance may be legally downloaded from www.folkways.si.edu on the album *Seneca Social Dance Music,* performed by Avery and Fidelia Jimerson. The name is said to relate to an old custom where dancers propped their quivers against one another by stoves at either end of the Longhouse. At one time, it was the first and the last dance. The quivers were counted to ensure that all men had come back home from battle. The dancers circle counterclockwise around both stoves. Everyone falls into one long single-file line and does a gentle, flat-foot jog with a slight dip to one side. It is a good way to warm up.

The next dance is generally a Moccasin Dance (similar to the Fish Dance), accompanied by the water drum and cow-horn rattles, like the majority of social dances. This dance has a faster tempo and a twisting dance step.

After that, the order of the dances varies. Someone will act as "push" or master of ceremonies, choosing who will sing next and which of the more than two dozen varieties of Iroquois social dances will be performed. With few exceptions, the dancing moves counterclockwise in a circle around the singers' benches. There are social dances named after animals as common as the rabbit or as exotic (relative to southern Ontario and New York State) as the alligator, dances with ambiguous names such as Strike-the-Stick, and dances that imply the sociality of the event, such as the Friendship Dance. Certain dances are not appropriate at the social: for example, the showy Smoke Dance that is increasingly a favorite competition dance at powwows.

The social dance tradition has welcomed new dance types from neighboring nations, including the Alligator Dance from the Seminole of Florida, the Round Dance brought north from Oklahoma, where a group of Seneca and Cayuga were moved in the nineteenth century, and the Shake the Bush Dance from the Tutelo, who lived alongside the Six Nations community. Levine notes that the Haudenosaunee Alligator Dance song uses a musical structure also heard in other Woodland social dance repertoires, including the Shawnee and Delaware Go Get 'Em Dance, the Yuchi Turtle Dance, the Caddo and Shawnee Alligator Dance, and the Choctaw Quail Dance (Jackson and Levine 2000).

Occasionally, the events may stop to make a space for invited guests from another nation. At this point, a dance might be done that is normally not part of the social. But here, too, protocol must be followed.

Sadie emphasizes that the associations and context of the different types of music are important but not all the younger singers have that knowledge. Where did you hear it before? Who made it? Those sorts of information are meaningful. The social affirms the connectedness of the Haudenosaunee to the birds and animals, as well as to their fellow dancers and singers. It recognizes the responsibility of humans to help celebrate life. "There's no such thing as a good singer. It's the job they have to do… The strength you get out of the song, that's what makes people want to dance," Sadie explains. It's inevitably a joyous evening.

INTRODUCING THE HAUDENOSAUNEE

The Haudenosaunee are members of the nations that were historically called the Iroquois. They call themselves *Ongwehonwe*, a word that means "real people." They live in fourteen communities mostly in New York State, southern Ontario, and Quebec (Figure 4.3), although there is a community of Oneida in Wisconsin and Oklahoma Seneca and Cayuga most of whom were removed from their lands in Ohio in the wake of Andrew Jackson's Removal Bill of 1830.

Metaphorically, their lands are a longhouse, with the Mohawk as the "western door," the Oneida, next, the Onondaga as the "firekeepers" in the center of the territory, and then the Cayuga and finally the Seneca at the "eastern door." The Oneida and Cayuga are referred to as the "little brothers." The League of the Iroquois, as some textbooks refer to them, brought in the Tuscarora via the Cayuga in 1714 as another younger brother in the longhouse. It was a process of "extending the rafters," a phrase that indicates the mechanism by which newcomers can be incorporated. While some communities may consist predominantly of one nation, others (the community of Six Nations in Ontario, for instance) may have residents from several of the six nations, each with their own Longhouse.

Chapter 1 referred to traditional teachings of the Haudenosaunee, particularly the Great Law of Peace, which established a form of government as well as a structure of behavior and belief that enabled one of the strongest confederacies of nations to remain both culturally and politically powerful for many centuries, right to the present day. The political structure of the Iroquois Confederacy was so impressive that Thomas Jefferson consulted with Iroquois leaders, and many believe (see Grinde 1995, for instance) that he borrowed a number of elements in devising a constitution for the new nation of the United States. The system balances the responsibilities of the different member nations, as well as of men and women. While fifty men constitute the circle of hereditary chiefs who are charged with decision making, it is the clan mothers who "raise up" and advise those chiefs. Various elements of contemporary culture existed before and after the time of the Peacekeeper who brought the Great Law, as the historical chart (Figure 1.6) in Chapter 1 demonstrated.

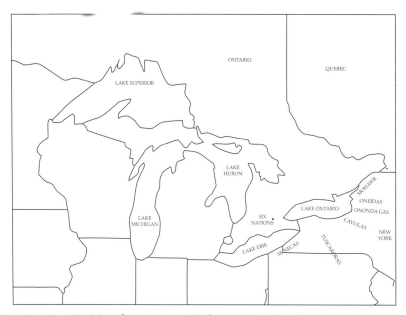

FIGURE 4.3   *Map of contemporary Haudenosaunee First Nations.*

There have been a few cultural renewals, including one associated with Handsome Lake, whose "Code" was also discussed in Chapter 1. It was his text that laid the groundwork for the contemporary Longhouse religion.

The languages of the six nations are closely related and mutually intelligible but distinct in various ways. Sadie Buck explains that Seneca is rolling and smooth but Cayuga has more glottal stops, and singers often switch to Seneca because of that.

Each of the six nations undertakes an annual cycle of seasonal Longhouse ceremonies to honor Creation, just as the Thanksgiving Address does. Music and dance function in ceremonies as part of this honoring. While the structure of the annual cycle is generally similar, each community may embellish that structure, creating differences in the procedures of dressing, the sequences of events, and the format of each ceremony. Here, courtesy of Sadie Buck, is the annual ceremonial cycle of the Seneca Longhouse at the community of Six Nations in Ontario:

1. Maple and All-Tree Ceremony—Late February or early March.
2. Maple Syrup Harvest Ceremony—Late March or early April.
3. Thunder Ceremony—Early April after first thunder.
4. Feast of the Dead—Middle of April.
5. Medicine Mask Ceremony—End of April.
6. Sun Dance Ceremony—Early May.
7. Moon Dance Ceremony—Early May.
8. Seed Blessing Ceremony—Middle of May.
9. Planting Conclusion Ceremony—Middle of May.
10. Strawberry Festival—Middle of June.
11. Green Bean Festival—Early August.
12. Small Green Corn Dance—Middle of August.
13. Big Green Corn Dance—Late August (three days' duration).
14. Harvest Festival—Middle of October.
15. Medicine Mask Ceremony—Middle to late October.
16. Feast of the Dead—Late October.
17. Code of Handsome Lake—Late October or late November.
18. Midwinter Ceremony—January (five nights after the new moon; eight days' duration).

At the heart of Haudenosaunee life are clans. There are nine basic ones, but some of their names and configurations vary by community. Children inherit their clan from their mother. Clans are usually organized into two moieties, and these moiety divisions, along with gender, determine where one sits for different Longhouse "doings," or ceremonies. Historically, each clan had different responsibilities, and all are represented on the Confederacy council of chiefs. The social, political, and religious implications of clan affiliation, as well as the differences in local community practices, are complex matters. As Sam Cronk has written:

> A quick survey of literature about Iroquoian culture suggests that far more has been written about music at ceremonies and "doings" than at social occasions. But when I first talked with Iroquoian singers, I soon realized that many have strong concerns about non-Native interest in these fairly restricted and often quite personal events; some people question the need of the non-Native public to have access to information for which it has no practical use. Even within these communities, restrictions are in place to safeguard ceremonial and curing songs from misuse and exploitation. (1990, 30)

These are issues that students must carefully consider if they wish to learn more about belief and ceremony. If you want to begin to study further, you can find a great deal of published material. Reliable starting points are Annemarie Anrod Shimony's *Conservatism Among the Iroquois at the Six Nations Reserve* (1961/1994) or Michael Foster's *From the Earth to Beyond the Sky* (1974).

HAUDENOSAUNEE SINGERS AND SOCIAL DANCE SONGS

When I asked Sadie whom she would regard as an outstanding singer and song maker that we might honor in this text, she had a ready answer: Gordie Buck. As early as the 1950s, when the dance ethnographer Gertrude Kurath visited the Six Nations community, Kurath described him as an important Longhouse singer with a formidable repertoire (1968, 191). Gordie was singing by the age of five. Sadie stresses that Gordie's strong gift for music is "a strong indication of what music is in our life. It permeates his whole being. There's not a person who could say he didn't know music. That's how strong his gift was. He was a man who could do all the songs. He could lead anything. For Gordie, songs were like air." She tells a story of a visiting hoop dancer (from western Canada) whose singer didn't show up for a performance. The man wanted to dance, and so he sang his song through once to Gordie, and Gordie got up on stage and sang while the hoop dancer danced. Recently, Gordie has been awarded an Ontario Medal for Good Citizenship for his cultural contributions. Listen to this great singer perform a set of Women's Shuffle Dance songs (*Ęhsgá:nye:*) recorded by Sam Cronk in 1985 (CD track 15).

There have been many other notable singers. There are now many young groups of singers, both male and female. Well-known groups who have now made some of their repertoire available on CDs are the Six Nations Women Singers, Bill Crouse, the Allegany Singers, led by members of the Kyle Dowdy family, and the Old Mush Singers from Six Nations, organized in 1992 by Amos Key Jr., Hubert Buck Jr., and Steve Hill.

These singers perform various repertoires: social dance songs, ceremonial repertoires, and in some cases also medicine "doings." Sadie Buck explains that the vocal quality changes from one type of repertoire to the next. The *Ęhsgá:nye:* are sung with some "throaty" quality, although not the deep, throaty sound of medicine songs. By contrast, the *Qtǫ:wís:as*, women's thanksgiving songs for the Planting Ceremony, are performed with a high head tone. Individual voices vary a lot, of course, but good singers have the ability to change their vocal production for different repertoires. Social dance songs will be the focus here.

The "social dance song" label is not entirely satisfactory, since there is a purpose and a meaning to each dance that blurs the boundary between what is sacred and what is secular, as Sadie's comments about Gordie Buck make clear. Social dance songs are often described as "earth songs" because they were created here on earth. In Sadie Buck's words, "They are a celebration of your physical being." An elder from the community of Akwesasne, Dave Jock, offers a similar explanation: "We are singing for the earth and that's of course all of us. Every one of these songs is in that kind of respect. They come from the animal life; they come from the birds, they come from the sound of the wind. Everything that is alive is where these sounds come from. The waters, the way they flow, and the sound that they make. They are all singing something to keep the world and the life alive" (workshop presented at Queen's University, 1986). Some of the dances have been posted on youtube.

The social dance song genre that is central to the sing is the *Ehsgá:nye:* or Women's Shuffle Dance, as you learned earlier. While it is a genre that has both very old and very new compositions, many new ones are added to the repertoire each year, and skilled song leaders know many. Sadie Buck describes an occasion when she and Kyle Dowdy Sr. sang for over four hours, without running out of new songs.

Each song leader has his or her own favorite sets. Sadie stresses the importance of being "honorable" in the repertoire performed publically by "only singing songs that you know where they came from." Respect for the community is also evident in the role that singing groups play. The Six Nations Women Singers (Figure 4.4), for instance, is a "singing society," a type of mutual aid society. Any money they make through performance goes to a specific family in need or to a shared project. Singing societies often sell CDs to raise funds for community projects. Hence, both live performances and commodified ones may do the same work: helping the community.

I asked Sadie to choose one of her own songs to highlight in this chapter. She chose the *Ęhsgá:nye:* that is available on our iMix because

FIGURE 4.4   *Six Nations Women Singers. Back row (L-R): Charlene Bomberry, Sadie Buck, Betsy Buck; Front row (L-R) Pat Hess, Janice G. Martin, Jaynane Burning.   (Photo courtesy of Sadie Buck)*

it is "representative" of the genre in various ways: "That's right in the range of our throats, and that's right in the range of how we use our throats [for Ęhsgá:nye:] ... It's got the highs and the lows. Even though it's a simple melody it's got a little twist in there. It's got the glottals, the stops in your throat."

Each Ęhsgá:nye: song has two repetitions, as indicated on the transcription (Figure 4.5) of the composition by Sadie Buck.

/A—Lead singer   A—group   B—group / A—group   B—group/

ACTIVITY 4.1   *Listen to Sadie's* eskanye *(iMix) with particular attention to the phrase repetition patterns.*

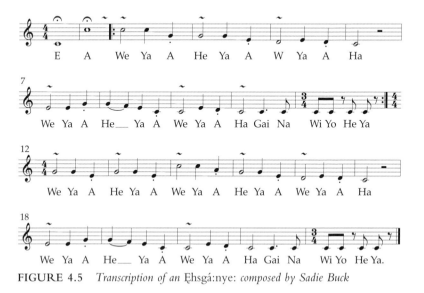

FIGURE 4.5   *Transcription of an* Ęhsgá:nye: *composed by Sadie Buck*

The text of this song consists entirely of vocables. The lead singer begins by resting momentarily on the highest note, waiting until everyone hears the rhythm and the pitch reference. The first iteration of phrase A is done solo and then the group repeats it. Each repetition of phrase B ends with the phrase "*gainawiyo heya*," vocables which mark virtually all *Ęhsgá:nye:*. This phrase often introduces a change of meter at the end of the phrase.

ACTIVITY 4.2 *Compare the* Ęhsgá:nye: *set (three songs) performed by Gordie Buck (CD track 15) and the single* Ęhsgá:nye: *by the Six Nations Women Singers (iMix #5). Focus on the characteristic phrase* "gainawiyo heya." *You will notice that an older singer such as Gordie Buck sometimes abbreviates the phrase, whereas the Six Nations Women Singers perform it more clearly and completely.*

The point where A is repeated by the group is marked by two shifts in the cow-horn rattle pattern, first a tremolo, and then a half-speed beat to "straighten out the beat," as the singers explain it. Different groups also have distinctive ending patterns played on the water drum. The Six Nations Women Singers, for instance, end with three half notes followed by three quarter notes. It also seems as if each group pitches its singing in a distinctive relationship to the clear pitch of the water drum. The Six Nations Women Singers most often sing a major second above the water drum pitch. Arguably, this gives their performance a distinctive harmonic edge.

ACTIVITY 4.3 *Listen to Sadie Buck's* Ęhsgá:nye: *again and try to hear the shifts in the rhythmic patterns of water drum and cow-horn rattles. Once you understand where to "straighten out the beat" and how to end the song, play the cow-horn rattle pattern along with the recording.*

While this *Ęhsgá:nye:* uses vocables only, many have a few words in one or both languages, Seneca/Cayuga and English. Sam Cronk has written that "some singers use English phrases as vocables choosing words for their sound or rhythmic quality, rather than their linguistic meaning" (1988, 53). As Sadie Buck says, "the beat is so intrinsic they can put anything in a song."

Perhaps this capacity for "putting anything in a song" also relates to a much-appreciated aspect of the *Ęhsgá:nye:* tradition: humor. When the Six Nations Women Singers recorded for the Smithsonian Institution's CD *Heartbeat of the Nation,* they chose to include "Bingo" (legally downloadable from www.folkways.si.edu).

> The gist of it is, "I've only got two dollars but I'm going to go to bingo anyway." That's funny but people do that. They spend their last dollars on bingo instead of buying a loaf of bread. Even though its intent is to laugh and make fun of that, if you're inclined, it makes you think. But, if you're not so inclined, it would make you laugh. It allows the person who's hearing it to have the thought, or the extension of the thought of it...It's really gentle. Because it's celebrating. You can't take it out of the context that it was created for: to be danced to. It's got to make you feel to dance. To make you want to feel to dance you've got to feel the music. (Sadie Buck, recorded discussion, March 2006)

There are a number of *Ęhsgá:nye:* relating to children's nursery rhymes. Sadie's father, Hubert Buck Sr., composed "Humpty Dumpty" and "Old Macdonald." Sadie explains the effect of switching languages in the former:

> It starts in Seneca: "We're going to sing this song about Humpty Dumpty." The gist is, "You all know what happened to him next." Then it switches to English and says, "He fell off the wall and now he's scrambled eggs." The switch from Seneca to English is the really funny part because, even if you perform it in front of a non-Haudenosaunee audience, they don't understand the first part but they hear the word Humpty Dumpty. Then the last part, "He fell off the wall and now he's scrambled eggs," you can hear the audience laugh. It's interesting because sometimes the audience doesn't laugh right away. They're thinking, "What does that song say? They're singing in English." All of that goes into the humor of that song. (ibid.)

Sadie herself contributed "Mary Had a Little Lamb," an *Ęhsgá:nye:* that is completely in English. The final line, "It followed her to school one day and got better marks than her," has the comic twist. Another *Ęhsgá:nye:* relating to children's lore is "Peter Cottontail" (CD track 16), composed by Alfred Key and Floyd Harris and performed by the Old Mush Singers.

In earlier generations, cowboy songs were popular influences and sources of quotations in *Ęhsgá:nye:* songs. On Smithsonian Folkways *Songs and Dances of the Great Lakes Indians,* on a track entitled "Women's Dance," a song of an earlier generation, composed by Huron Miller, "My Son Calls Another Man Daddy," was made available. It may be legally downloaded from www.folkways.si.edu.

Cronk writes about other humorous aspects of the *Ęhsgá:nye:* tradition:

> Some feature musical "jokes," such as unexpected silences part way through a song. Texts might be comic, such as the "Indian Beatles" eskanyeh, recognizing the impact of rock and roll. Many songs provide a wry social commentary; for example, a recent example from Akwesasne, New York, ends with: "Cigarettes, bingo, gasoline! What's this world coming to? *Gai no wi ha:h, he ya…*" Through eskanyeh, singers are able to address the very serious issues which confront their community. Humour provides a way of releasing tension, of "putting things in proper perspective"—It is a gift that many Longhouse singers share." (1988, 53)

The Women's Shuffle Dance step is hard to describe in words. It is done by women only, as you might expect from the English name, and all dancers keep their feet close to the ground. Some dancers explain that you must keep in contact with Mother Earth throughout. Sadie explains that you must make it smooth, and she describes how she is constantly looking for good dancing shoes with hard soles that move without too much friction. Sneakers make it hard! The feet twist from side to side, inching forward around the counterclockwise circle. The proper motion is a sliding and dragging motion, but some younger dancers tend to push the feet. Linguist Amos Key Jr. explains that the tempos got much faster starting in the 1930s (personal communication, 1986). Before that, people used to say that you drew rhythms with your feet, but now the song is too fast for that.

Why has the *Ęhsgá:nye:* remained the favorite genre for new song creation? One reason is likely that it has been able to reflect both the traditional and the contemporary—the centuries-old form, as well as new tunes, new subject matter, and current ideas about social relationships both within the nation and between nations.

Of the dozens of other earth songs, there is space here to discuss only a few. These include dances that mimic birds or animals, such as the Rabbit, Robin, and Duck Dances, as well as the Round Dance, the competitive Smoke Dance, and the "Unity Stomp."

Some came to the Northeast from other regions. A popular couple dance is the Rabbit Dance, said to have been brought by Chauncey Isaacs and Percy Smoke from Oklahoma in the late 1950s. The dance step is similar to the Cherokee two-step. When Gertrude Kurath was doing research in the community of Six Nations in the late 1950s she noted, "There are rumors of its inclusion in social dances, though I have not seen it on the Reserve" (Kurath 1968, 192). That had certainly changed a few decades later.

Partners face one another and hold hands with arms crossed, so that right hands are joined and left hands are joined. The couple takes two side steps in one direction, often circling with their hands to follow their feet, and then one step back. This creates a three-beat dance rhythm. Arguably, it also mimics the somewhat erratic motions of the rabbit. And since it is a couple dance, there is a hint of courtship possibilities. The Rabbit Dance songs, however, do not parallel the dance pattern in three. There is a pleasureable tension between the rhythm of the dance and the rhythm of the song. (See our iMix #6.)

In the Robin Dance, people sidestep around the circle to mimic the bird that is often the earliest sign of spring. The song has an extra beat at one point, and here, the dancers turn and face the opposite direction. The Duck Dance and Pigeon Dance are also associated with spring. The Duck Dance always evokes laughter. A double line of men move forward to meet a double line of women. They "push" the women backwards by walking toward them as the current might push a duck on the water. At a certain point, the men raise their arms and the women duck underneath. But those arms quite often fall again and "capture" a pair of women.

The Round Dance is a welcoming dance in which men and women sometimes dance in separate circles. One explanation of the meaning is that the outer circle moves in the traditional Haudenosaunee direction, counterclockwise, the direction of life on earth. But the circles change direction in the course of the song. This is the only time in the context of a social that Haudenosaunee dance in the other direction, and this is said to mirror the direction of dance in the spirit world.

Another category of dance is competitive. The Smoke Dance is the most popular of these and has now become a staple part of powwows in the Northeast and sometimes elsewhere. The fast tempo and complicated footwork are dazzling but difficult. Kyle Dowdy Sr. explains that the Smoke Dance was created when singers speeded up old war dance songs. His group, the Allegany Singers, have recorded some of these songs (CD track 17), first sung slowly and then at the fast tempo.

> **ACTIVITY 4.4** *Listen to CD track 17, noting the tempo change and comparing the melodic contour of the slow and fast versions.*

At the outset of this chapter, we described how the song genre that opened the social on the evening of the sing was a Standing Quiver Dance, a type of stomp dance. There are various other types of stomp dance used by different First Nations along the Atlantic seaboard. We know that the Haudenosaunee had *Gada:tro:t* long before some of their members were removed to Oklahoma. But new stomp dances were learned from their neighbors there, including the Cherokee and the Shawnee, who had also been removed from lands further east. One genre of Haudenosaunee social dance is the Cherokee Stomp Dance. When performed in the Southeast, however, the Cherokee dance has a sound very different from the Haudenosaunee stomp dance songs. Some Cherokee Stomp Dance songs have been released by Indian House Records.

The Southeastern (Cherokee or Creek) women dance with turtle-shell rattles tied on their calves a little below the knee, or, in recent times, perhaps tin cans (as many as twenty per leg) filled with fine rattling material. As they shuffle forward, the sound is a gentle one, perhaps like sand shifting on the shore or fine ice particles. Cherokee folklorist and historian Rayna Green has described the Southeastern stomp dance as follows:

> The women make the rattles, called shackles, out of box turtles—sometimes condensed milk tins—sewn onto pieces of leather. Nowadays, they're just as likely to be sewn on the top parts of old cowboy boots. I told a friend who was making a pair that she must have had to mesmerize that cowboy so she could skin him out like that! The shackles are heavy and the people dance all night, but the shell-shakers keep the beat…The members of the Keetoowah Society keep the stompgrounds because they keep the Sacred Fire, including the Principal Fire and all those fires taken to other places in Oklahoma. The Keetoowahs help the Aniyunwiya remember. The people who belong to the stompgrounds sit under their seven brush arbors. Things begin when they are all represented, and everybody else rings around that huge circle. At particular celebrations, the people might play stickball and make a speech telling the history of the People

and this stompground. After playing ball and sharing food, they dance...People come from the outside rings and inside to join the counterclockwise movement of a particular dance. They dance all night. There are lots of stomp dances; some are about animals, others about friendship, even love. These are always happy dances. Sometimes the song tells a funny story and laughter rises up in the middle of the dance. You should hear what Rabbit sang when he taught the wolves a new dance...At the end, Cherokees might say *wado, wado,* thank you, because they have so appreciated the song and the dance. So that's what I'll say because it made me happy to tell about the Stomp Dance. (In Heth 1992, 177)

Another stomp dance is the "Unity Stomp," so named because it uses stylistic elements from different First Nations' traditions as the call-and-response patterns change. Some segments are very short and narrow ranged, others longer and more expansive melodically. Unlike the Standing Quiver Dance, the Unity Stomp often moves freely through indoor and outdoor spaces, perhaps coiling and uncoiling, in an action that suggests a connection to the Mi'kmaq Snake Dance discussed in Chapter 3.

The "Unity Stomp" performed by the Six Nations Women Singers has been shared with the Six Nations–born rock musician Robbie Robertson. He weaves his song about coming back to his own community around the "Unity Stomp," performed by the Six Nations Women Singers. Their Unity Stomp may be accessed in our iMix (#7).

ACTIVITY 4.5   *Listen to Robbie Robertson and the Six Nations Women Singers perform the Unity Stomp. Learn some of the responses in the traditional segments and sing along. Listen carefully to Robertson's text for words that you have learned in this chapter:* Ongwehonwe, *for instance.*

TRADITIONAL KNOWLEDGE AND MODERNITY: CONTEMPORARY ADAPTATIONS OF SOCIAL DANCE SONGS

The Robbie Robertson song already introduces the topic of adapting social dance songs. Using traditional elements in modern arrangements raises a huge issue for Haudenosaunee and all other indigenous people. Robertson's arrangement employs one strategy for developing new artistic work out of older tradition. The two styles are layered but remain quite separate from one another. The result is that we think about the journey of a modern musician such as Robertson in relation to the tradition he came from without any hint that he has taken that tradition from the community. The Six Nations Women Singers feel that he respects the tradition because he has not changed the "context" of their song.

The concept of fusing styles is, of course, a very commonplace one in the late twentieth century and early twenty-first century. Many scholars and musicians have debated what this "fusion" really means. Steven Feld, for instance, has suggested that references to tradition are "safe genre statements of authenticity" (1994, 270). Lipsitz (1994) has described them as "dangerous crossroads" where the potential for political alliance and artistic innovation may be threatening to power brokers who want to keep everyone in their place.

Sadie Buck offers a thoughtful Haudenosaunee perspective on the issue of fusion. In contrast to definitions she frequently hears, describing fusion in mechanical terms as "putting elements together," she sees fusion as something deeper: "You hear that music and take it into yourself, and then it will come out differently. It happens at a core level, not a mechanical one. It's really innovation, not superficially putting elements together."

Sadie Buck herself is no stranger to fusion. Indeed, she explains that fusion is the only means by which contemporary artists can actually own their work, since the traditional songs belong to her nation. One of her largest projects to date is the opera *BONES*, created at the Banff Centre for the Arts in Alberta, where she had directed the Aboriginal Women's Voices program in the late 1990s. This work will be discussed in Chapter 5, where the concepts of hybridity and fusion will be elaborated in relation to other sorts of contemporary music.

Rather similar to Sadie's vision of fusion is the work of Ulali (who will be introduced more fully in the next chapter). While the roots of Ulali's members are diverse—Pura Fe is Tuscaroran and her musical heritage has been extensively jazz related; Soni Moreno has Mayan, Latino, and Apache roots; Jennifer Kreisberg is part Tuscaroran—they know the social dances of the Tuscarora, Eastern Cherokee, and other Atlantic seaboard tribes of the Southeast. They do a series of stomp dances (CD track 18) on their CD, *Makh Jchi*. The traditional turtle rattlers tied to the legs of dancers are now replaced by small, handheld shakers with fine-grained material such as sand. The call-and-response patterns are retained, but the responses are harmonized with closely spaced triadic patterns and smoothly coordinated glides into new keys. The rhythms grow out of the asymmetries of the traditional songs, now inflected with syncopations that evoke Pura Fe's jazz background or perhaps Soni's Latin American heritage.

For other artists, on the other hand, fusion may be a matter of re-interpreting and recontextualizing traditional elements. The popular Oneida singer Joanne Shenandoah's work is a case in point. Usually described as a New Age artist, Joanne has now created many CDs that use elements of her roots. Recently she made a musical series about the important teachings described in Chapter 1: the creation story and peacemaker's journey. When she records the "Rabbit Dance" that the Six Nations Women Singers perform on our iMix (#8), for instance, she renames it "Messenger" (on the album *Life Blood*). The exact tune is performed in a much slower tempo with synthesizer accompaniment and a gentle vocal manner.

ACTIVITY 4.6 *Listen again to the traditional performance of a Rabbit Dance (iMix #6), and then to Shenandoah's New Age arrangement of the same song (iMix #8). Note the differences between them, both those outlined in the previous paragraph and any additional ones that you can hear.*

One of her award-winning recording projects, *Matriarch*, incorporated some elements of *Ęhsgá:nye:* in combination with stylistic aspects of other musical genres from various parts of the world. She made one song for various female relatives and friends, using the traditional form but adding harmony, flute, various percussion, and guitar parts to reflect some aspects of the personality of the dedicatee in the arrangement. Most of Joanne Shenandoah's recordings can be legally downloaded from iTunes.

The differences in definition of hybridity, fusion, and appropriation are central to the ongoing and ever-changing construction of contemporary indigenous identities. Not everyone agrees about which of the examples that we have just discussed are respectful. Opinions may relate to pragmatic matters such as who is credited with the creation of a song, or who benefits financially from its recording. They may also relate to the way in which traditional contexts are preserved or not.

IROQUOIS HYMNS

While thus far we have discussed Haudenosaunee social structures, dance, and song practices that relate to traditional followers of the Longhouse religion, many members of the Iroquois nations are Christian. As we have seen in other regions and communities, hymns have often been adapted both musically and socially. French Jesuit missionaries arrived first in what is now Quebec, establishing mission villages that would become the Mohawk communities of Kahnawake, Kanasatake, and St. Regis. Episcopal and Methodist ministers, including the Mississauga chief Peter Jones (d. 1852), had some influence in New York and Ontario.

Oneida hymn singers in Ontario, for instance, function much like the traditional Singing Societies described above. Such groups may have emerged from the tradition of eighteenth- and nineteenth-century singing schools, since some of the repertoire that is still maintained uses that style. Combinations of triads and open fifths, chords mostly in root position, and rugged voice leading that sometimes has dramatic leaps—features that American studies students are more likely to associate with William Billings or Sacred Harp singing—characterize some of the repertoire they perform (see Diamond 1986). Oneida hymn singers also enjoy gospel songs, especially ones with call-and-response refrains. One such example, "On the Beautiful Beyond," is performed by Oneida from Green Bay, Wisconsin, and may be heard on www.folkways.si.edu.

TRADITIONAL KNOWLEDGE AND ENCOUNTER

Like the Atlantic seaboard nations, the Haudenosaunee have a long history of interaction with both colonizers and other First Nations. Their powerful political, social, and spiritual teachings as well as the various moments of renewal (particularly with the arrival of the Peacemaker and, later, the visionary Handsome Lake) have enabled this confederacy of nations to remain strong. They withstood land loss, especially in the eighteenth century, negotiated a place of neutrality in various European wars (although some Haudenosaunee chose to be allied with the British), welcomed the brotherhood of Tuscarora as well as Delaware and Tutelo who moved to share their lands. In some cases, as with the Six Nations community in southern Ontario, they secured a land grant that has given them a permanent place (although there have been land losses here as well). Even as this book was being written, a confrontation was

ongoing between developers and the Six Nations community over
the boundaries of Haudenosaunee land. At times, they have endured
displacement: some Oneida moved to Wisconsin and some Cayuga and
Seneca were resettled in Oklahoma. They saw their chiefs arrested in
1924 when the Canadian government imposed elected councils on their
communites. In the 1960s, the Kinzua Dam project flooded Allegany
lands and forced the resettlement of over one hundred families.

Through these challenges and many others, they have remained
strong. Although some traditions have shifted in popularity from one
decade to another, as in any dynamic society, the ceremonies and the
social dance traditions that enable traditionalists regularly to offer
thanks for those things that sustain life have never been lost. In the late
twentieth century, immersion schools in many communities enabled a
strengthening of indigenous languages and demonstrated that children
trained in their mother tongue excel academically and professionally.
Haudenosaunee leaders play major leadership roles in the revitalization
of First Nations culture and in the ongoing development of policy for
Aboriginal people in both Canada and the United States.

CHAPTER 5

Contemporary Intertribal and Cross-Cultural Native American Music

Previous chapters have made the point that indigenous music constantly develops and changes. Traditional song genres are sometimes carefully maintained in older forms, but often they are recontextualized or fused with contemporary popular idioms. The discourses that surround these contemporary uses of tradition often reflect contested definitions of identity, and they articulate responses to colonialism or to other historical or contemporary social issues. The hybrid examples discussed earlier demonstrate that the traditional and contemporary are not chronologically separate realms. Indeed, music that has come to be labeled "traditional" often accommodates new styles and songs, while some of the oldest repertoires continue to function within Native American modernity.

This chapter seeks to explore artistic work, including theater, that is explicitly intertribal and cross-cultural. The themes of encounter and modernity are of central concern. Those themes relate, in part, to the ways that mainstream norms, aesthetics, and industry structures constrain and position Native American performers and performing artists. With reference to a different indigenous tradition (that of Aboriginal people of Australia), Peter Dunbar-Hall and Christopher Gibson (2004) describe the challenges of modern musical indigeneity using Penny van Toorn's 1990 concept of "patron discourse." They define patron discourse as "a set of normative expectations and ways of listening in non-Aboriginal society, within which minority voices must struggle for audience" (2004, 25). In relation to the themes of encounter and modernity, this issue is relevant to the musicians considered in this chapter. How do mainstream listening expectations shape their positioning? In addition, however, how and why do First Nations, Inuit, and Métis artists accept, refuse, or selectively adopt mainstream aesthetics? Underlying all of this is arguably a more interesting question: is there a mainstream at all, in North American society of the twenty-first century?

Intertribal and cross-cultural Native American and Inuit music flourished in the late twentieth century partially because of changes in technology and communications transmission. While commodification is not a new practice, the last decades of the twentieth century saw a distinct burgeoning of audio and video recordings, made possible by less-expensive equipment for production and new means of circulation, particularly the Internet. The development of "Rez radio," as well as television networks such as the nationwide Aboriginal Peoples Television Network in Canada, has also helped create a cultural renaissance since approximately the 1980s. A recent discography, Brian Wright-McLeod's *Encyclopedia of Native Music* (2005), lists more than 1800 CDs currently available. The subdivisions of his book indicate many sorts of musical practices that have been put into broader intercultural circulation in the late twentieth and early twenty-first centuries. In addition to many varieties of traditional music, Wright-McLeod lists powwow, flute, chicken scratch (though not in the region that this book is discussing), peyote ritual music (not widely practiced in the region that this book is discussing), and many genres of popular music. The remainder of this chapter will look at two kinds of intertribal and intercultural musical activity: powwow and popular music, both of which have been commodified and circulated beyond local communities and national borders.

POWWOWS IN EASTERN NORTH AMERICA

While the powwow arrived rather recently in the regions that this volume is foregrounding, it plays such an important role in recent decades that this book would be remiss without considering it. Furthermore, while a number of recent powwow studies (Ellis et al. 2005, Goertzen 2001, Hoefnagels 2001) emphasize the localization of powwow practices, many powwow histories (Hoefnagels is an exception) do not yet acknowledge the spread of the tradition in the Northeast. So this chapter attempts partially to fill a lacuna. There are a growing number of drums based in Atlantic Canada and New England. One of the earliest was the Mi'kmaq Birch Creek Singers, who brought the big drum tradition to the region. Since the 1990s, many other groups, such as the Eastern Eagle Singers (Nova Scotia Mi'kmaq), the Sipu'jij Drummers (Newfoundland Mi'kmaq), Indian Bay Singers (Nova Scotia Mi'kmaq), and Spirit of the Dawn (Maine Penobscot), are active in eastern Canada and the United States.

There are many different stories about the origins of the contemporary powwow. Most historians trace the roots to the male warrior societies of the southern Plains (such as the Hethuska of the Omaha/Ponca, or the Pawnee Iruska Society). The Kiowa Gourd Dance was another important influence. Luke Lassiter (1998) documents the revitalization of this dance in southern Oklahoma since the 1970s. With the enforced removal of many eastern communities to reserves in Oklahoma, intertribal exchange intensified. The powwow spread from the southern Plains west to the Sioux and then north to the Ojibwe, Cree, Blood, Assiniboine, Blackfoot, and others after the 1950s, eventually moving northeast in the last two decades of the twentieth century. Along the way, elements of other local practices—the Ojibwe Drum Dance tradition (see Vennum 1982), for instance, or Haudenosaunee competitive Smoke Dance contests (described in Chapter 4)—were absorbed.

Powwows were often mapped onto colonial events. In the late nineteenth century, bans on Indian dancing were legislated in both the United States and Canada. Various restrictive acts of legislation were not fully repealed until the 1960s. But Indian dances were often allowed in government- or church-defined contexts. Late nineteenth-century "Treaty Day" celebrations or visits by government officials in northern Ontario, for instance, included dancing with the big drum (see, e.g., Diamond et al. 1994, 31).

Gatherings in association with fairs, athletic contests, or church-sponsored events were among other antecedents in the Northeast. Describing the history of powwows in southwestern Ontario, Anna Hoefnagels notes:

> As precursors to powwows, camp meetings functioned as large social gatherings for Native people from neighbouring communities, albeit with heavy Christian overtones with prayer and singing, and efforts to convert the Native people in attendance. The connection between the origins of powwows with Christian community churches is also evident in the history of the Walpole Island event, as this gathering evolved out of staged dance performances that were held as fund-raisers for the community Anglican Church. (2001, 97)

Intertribal sharing led, nonetheless, to the development of a format that became more or less standardized in different places. By 1955, the diffusion of powwows was so extensive that James Howard (1983) described it as a "pan-Indian" event and implied the demise of locally distinctive gatherings. All events feature the large horizontal frame drum, played by a group of singer-drummers, often called "the heartbeat" of the nations. All events include elements of regalia and dance steps that are similar (see "Powwow Fundamentals," below), and there is a great deal of repertoire swapping on the powwow circuit. Most powwows are competitive events, although there are many smaller, local, noncompetitive events, usually called "traditional" powwows. Virtually all are intertribal, often with participants from dozens of different nations. The audio examples in our iMix were all recorded live at annual Gathering of Nations powwows, one of the largest events involving both northern- and southern-style drums. All Gathering of Nations CDs may be legally downloaded from iTunes.

Many participants have contested the "pan-Indian" label, however, observing how powwows in different regions may be intertribal and yet retain or incorporate local features, including nation-specific dance types and "specials" that allow each event to function differently. As Choctaw ethnomusicologist Tara Browner has observed:

> Although admittedly pow-wows do contain elements of theatre—especially the competitive events—they are far more complex musically and socially than Howard is willing to concede. For whatever reasons, he and many other writers before 1990 insisted that in order for any Indian event to be musically and kinesthetically "authentic," participants had to embrace an aesthetic similar to that found in the rendezvous encampments of the American Mountain Man Society. In that group, no article of clothing or weapon can be displayed that came into use as a trade good after 1840. Powwow participants, however, are not like Civil War re-enactors. Although they dance and sing in ways drawn from historical tradition, they do so in the present—and to serve contemporary purposes and needs. (2002, 2)

Local differences have always marked the development of powwows and continue to be evident in contemporary events. The names of dances may differ, for instance. The anglicized word "powwow" itself is derived from an Algonquian-language word relating to "medicine person," but various names for intertribal gatherings were (and in some cases still are) used locally. The "war" dances of some nations were called, by more northern communities, the "Omaha" or "grass" dances.

The contemporary purposes and needs that Browner emphasizes may be served by "specials" held at a powwow to mark particular relationships or to help out someone in need. At one recent powwow, a blanket dance was announced in aid of a young boy who was seriously ill. Donations were contributed on a blanket in the center of the dance floor, as the family watched with tears and gratitude. At one community a few years earlier, a special ceremony was held to induct a young woman into the Jingle Dance Society (see "Powwow Fundamentals," below) of the Anishnabe people. At another powwow, following the tragic shooting of an Anishnabe man by police (in a case that is not totally resolved at the time of writing this text), the local powwow organizers held a special to reconcile the indigenous and non-indigenous attendees. In ways such as these, the powwow can address specific local needs at a specific point of time.

More generally, the purposes and needs served by powwows relate to the honoring of traditional values as well as kinship and intercommunity ties. As Lynn F. Hueneman has observed, "The main purpose may be social, but civil and even religious ceremonial elements remain important, such as honoring a veteran or other person with honor songs, or receiving a family back into public life after a period of mourning (in Heth 1992, 111). Those who are given special roles, for example sponsor, head dancer, flag bearer, emcee, or princess, learn responsibilities of various types. In the significant feasting and giveaway phases of a powwow, the importance of generosity is affirmed. Proper behavior is emphasized (as discussed below in relation to "protocol").

Anishnabe playwright Drew Hayden Taylor describes the function of powwows more informally:

> ...the reasons First Nations people go to powwows haven't changed all that much. For most of those who are not involved in the actual planning and running of the gatherings, it's essentially a chance to hang out, meet old friends, maybe make some new ones and revitalize their T-shirt collections. And where else can you get a buffalo burger, some corn soup and maybe some deer stew in today's fast-food world? Contrary to popular belief, the vast majority of native people, especially those who live in urban areas, do not stock their refrigerators with wild meat. (2004, 57)

Hayden Taylor gently asks, on the other hand, what may motivate non-Native attendees:

> Is it to look at all the exotic native people? I hope not. To tell you the truth, we're not that exotic. Whenever I'm on the reserve, I watch "Friends" and "Star Trek" while eating potato chips. Maybe they go to watch the dancing and listen to the drumming. I sometimes go for that. Yet I'm fairly sure that many of the people who are interested in native dance seldom go out to see some of their own uniquely cultural dances such as ballet, for instance. Granted powwow tickets are cheaper... (ibid.)

He is well aware that while there are important spiritual dimensions of powwows, many events welcome tourists and some, such as the annual Canadian Aboriginal Festival in Toronto, are major business opportunities not only for craft people, but also for institutions that seek to recruit native youth for college programs or jobs. Today, powwows may be hosted by First Nations communities, universities, casinos, or other businesses.

Many singers, dancers, and handicraft dealers spend their summer on the "powwow trail" moving from one competitive event to another. Dancers vie for prize money to cover their travel expenses. One powwow calendar for 2006 (Hutchens 2006) claims sales of over 75,000 and lists upwards of thirty events on a single weekend in North America but also in other countries such as Argentina, France, and Germany. Such regional (or intercontinental) powwow guides or Internet listings (see, e.g., www.powwow.com) are widely consulted for information about events in specific areas. There are even powwow cruises, in the early twenty-first century (www.powwowcruise.com). The international diffusion of the powwow has kept pace with the globalization of music more generally since the 1990s.

ACTIVITY 5.1   *Do an Internet search for powwows in the region where you live. Determine the host nation and drum of each event. Check to see whether the lead drum groups have made any recordings. Compare the information given for different events.*

POWWOW FUNDAMENTALS

The powwow grounds often resemble a series of concentric circles, although the physical layout is necessarily different depending on the configuration of space available in different settings. The drums are most often in the center. At outdoor powwows in the Northeast, the drums are under an arbor (often with a roof of boughs to protect them from the elements (Figure 5.1)). The circle of dancers surrounds the central arbor. Around them are families, elders, and other audience members who support the dancers. The audience is next, and then the concessions, with crafts, food, and lots of CDs.

The general sequence of events at powwows is familiar from one to another. Both northern and southern powwows begin with a Grand Entry. Flag bearers, war veterans, sometimes a powwow princess, male and female lead dancers, and then a stream of dancers of all ages—

FIGURE 5.1 *Powwow grounds with central drum arbor and Men's Traditional Dancers.* *(Photo by B. Diamond)*

from dozens of different First Nations, in some cases, organized in each of the competitive dance categories, with older dancers leading each group—all enter through the eastern door of the powwow circle and move clockwise around the dance area. Competitions for different age groups, starting with preschoolers, are scheduled as the day unfolds. Intertribal Dances are interspersed so that all dancers and also often audience members may join the drum circle.

The intense singing style of a group of men around a powwow drum has arguably become iconic of an undifferentiated Indian identity, for many newcomers to this tradition. A general distinction, however, is usually made between the southern and northern powwows and their styles of singing. The tempos (northern style uses slower tempos), vocal timbre (northern style is more intense and heavily "pulsated"), and details of dance regalia differ. The northern style is often described as more exuberant, while the southern is more restrained. The groups that are usually referred to as "northern" are the Lakota and Dakota, as well as the Northern Cree and the Ojibwe of the Canadian Plains. The northeastern drums of central and eastern Canada, as well as the Atlantic seaboard, on the other hand, may use vocal production that is less intense, nuanced by local singing traditions. Regalia may include objects or beadwork patterns that refelect one's community or specific First Nations identity. As a result, various people are starting to contest the distinction of northern and southern styles as an oversimplification.

ACTIVITY 5.2   *Listen to iMix #9 and #10, with excerpts of singing from three different powwow groups. The first, Sizzortail, is a southern-style drum, the second, Red Bull a northern-style drum. How might you describe differences and similarities in the timbre, or vocal quality? Compare the tempi. Listen again to the Mi'kmaq drum Eastern Eagle (iMix #4). How would you characterize their sound in relation to the southern and northern styles?*

In all regions, there are certain expectations about lifestyle that are associated with the powwow. Alcohol and drugs are not permitted in the vicinity of a powwow, and drummers are encouraged to abstain from these substances. Because of the cross-cultural audiences that attend powwows, the emcee often explains "protocols" for respectful behavior. The organizers may also publish such protocols on the Internet, where you will also find numerous histories of the different dance categories. Sometimes the emcee, whose job it is to keep the events moving and to share useful information with the attendees, will reiterate these rules and these histories in his commentary. He has an important role to play, always with good humor and encouragement for the dancers.

ACTIVITY 5.3   *Go online and enter "powwow protocol" in your favorite search engine to observe how non-Native audience members are taught how to act respectfully. If you do not find descriptions of dance styles on the websites you locate, do another search for "powwow dance styles." Pick one dance type, such as the Jingle Dress Dance, and compare the information that is currently online. How might you explain differences in the origin stories or the meanings associated with the metal cones on a jingle dress?*

Other than the Intertribals, northern dance types are gender specific. They include Men's Traditional Dance, Men's Grass Dance, and Men's Fancy Dance, Women's Traditional Dance, Women's Jingle Dress Dance, and Women's Fancy or Shawl Dance. The regalia, dance steps, song repertoires, and histories of each dance type are distinctive, as you learned by your Internet search. The origin stories of different dance types also frequently vary from one region to another.

Men's Traditional Dancers (see Figure 5.1) may wear the long belted shirt of southern Straight Dancers, but more often their regalia has a large eagle feather bustle made of natural feathers, attached to their waist at the back, ankle bells, a porcupine hair roach, and apron. Though a "pat-step" dance step is basic to this style, the dance movements may be quite individual, sometimes enacting movements of birds or animals, or movements relating to stalking and hunting an animal. The songs for Men's Traditional Dancing contain some of the most varied rhythms and phrase patterns of any powwow songs.

> **ACTIVITY 5.4** *The melody of the Men's Traditional song in our iMix (#12) is rhythmically quite varied. Compare this to the Intertribal in the iMix, #11, a song with less rhythmic complexity.*

A Grass Dancer (Figure 5.2), on the other hand, often outlines a circle with one foot, and the rotation of his body causes the long strands of yarn and ribbons on his regalia to sway. Grass Dance outfits have no bustle. This modern form of the Grass Dance became popular in northern powwows only in the 1980s even though its antecedent is regarded as one of the oldest dances of the Plains warrior societies. Some say it mirrors the stamping down of the high grass in the campground, while others refer to the tying of sweetgrass braids to dancers' belts.

Women Traditional Dancers (Figure 5.3) may wear buckskin or cloth dresses, often with traditionally embroidered collars and hems, or ribbon adornment, and they carry a folded fringed shawl over one arm. In some styles, they stand in one place and flex their knees to the music, causing the shawl fringe to move in rhythm. In other cases, they move elegantly and gracefully around the dance circle with small steps, always keeping their feet in contact with the earth. The tempo of their music is slower than that of other dance types (iMix #13)

The Jingle Dress Dance (Figure 5.4) is the newest addition to the powwow, arriving in the 1980s. In the Northeast, it is usually said to have originated among the Anishnabe of northern Ontario when an elder dreamed that dancing in this dress could heal his daughter who was seriously ill. The dress has many metal cones, originally made from snuff box or other tin can lids. Some say there should be 365 metal cones on a dress, one for each day of the year. The gentle sound of these jingling cones (iMix #14) contrasts markedly with the sound of any other powwow dance.

FIGURE 5.2 *Grass Dancer.* *(Photo by Franziska von Rosen. Used by permission.)*

ACTIVITY 5.5 *Listen to the Jingle Dress Dance song (iMix #14) and then listen to the Men's Fancy Dance song (iMix #15). The first has the sound of women's jingle dresses, while the second has the sound of leg bells. If you were a poet, what adjectives would you choose to describe the contrast between the two metallic timbres?*

Both the Men's and Women's Fancy Dances (Figures 5.5 and 5.6) are the fastest and most virtuosic of powwow dances. The men's out-fits have two colorful bustles at back, and many bright colors in the

FIGURE 5.3 *Women's Traditional Dancers.* *(Photo by B. Diamond.)*

beadwork, cloth, headbands, medallions, and decorative ribbons attached to the tips of feathers. The rapid footwork, jumps, spins, and dips in the men's dance are energetic and athletic. The drum tempo is the fastest of all the contemporary dances (iMix #15). The Women's Fancy Dance is also called a Shawl Dance, with reference to the fringed shawl that each dancer wears over the shoulders and holds with outstretched arms. Beaded calf-length moccasins and headband, carefully color coordinated, are also usually a part of this regalia. The dancer's movements also involve whirling and fast footwork, sometimes said to mimic a butterfly.

The powwow may also feature some other special dance types, including the Crow Hop, Sneak-Up Dance, Snake Dance, Forty-Niner, and Round Dance. Show dances such as the Hoop Dance may be included. In the East, social dances from the host nation are often interspersed. As mentioned in Chapter 4, the Haudenosaunee Smoke Dance

FIGURE 5.4   *Jingle Dress Dancers.*   *(Photo by B. Diamond.)*

is especially popular, but in Atlantic Canada, Mi'kmaq social dances are also frequently performed at powwows.

ACTIVITY 5.6   *See if your university library has a video of powwow dancing. Our resource list provides a number of titles. Watch a fifteen-minute (or longer) segment and try to distinguish the different types of regalia and different dance steps. Write a short essay describing the different dance moves you see as well as the variety of regalia in one or two of the dance categories.*

FIGURE 5.5   *Men's Fancy Dancers.*   *(Photo by B. Diamond.)*

ACTIVITY 5.7   *The competitive dance types described above are often distinguished by different tempos. Review the iMix powwow tracks to determine the tempo of each song type. Which is the fastest and which the slowest?*

The basic form of a powwow song is standardized, allowing singers from different nations or communities to perform together at times, and facilitating the exchange of repertoire. After a few drumbeats to establish the tempo, the lead singer begins in a high register with the first phrase. The sound is forceful and energetic. Some singers may pulsate the voice or use rough accents. The first phrase is repeated, or "seconded," by the rest of the group. The second and often the third phrases are closely related to the contour of the first phrase, but they start lower in pitch. The singers continue in unison, each subsequent phrase moving lower than the previous one, until the lowest note is reiterated to end the melody. The group then repeats the melody, omitting the A phrase. Ethnomusicologists have frequently described this form as "incomplete repetition form" and further noted that the melodic contour is "terraced." In powwow competition, there are often four repetitions, or "push-ups," of the

FIGURE 5.6   *Women's Shawl Dancer.*   *(Photo by B. Diamond.)*

whole song. The form might be written as follows, although the precise number of phrases following the A section is variable:

A (solo) A (group) ‖: BCD : ‖ [all repeated 4 times]

ACTIVITY 5.8   *Listen to iMix #15, and try to graph the phrases, using the same letter when a phrase repeats. Count the four push-ups. It may help to make a timing chart for the structure. Note which phrases are the longest and which the shortest. How exactly are the subsequent phrases melodically similar to phrase A?*

The form has sometimes been described in symbolic terms as a "call." There are various teachings about the symbolism of this song form. One Ontario Cree explanation is as follows:

> So the first part is the one where the leader sings. He comes on really high and he's alone and he starts off the song. That's the part where he calls on the Creator. That's what that part represents. He calls the Creator and says come and listen; we're gathered here the way you intended us.
>
> Then there's a second part when all the singers come in. And that one calls all the spirits of the animals and plants to come and listen—asks them to join in.
>
> And the third part calls on the men, people to come.
>
> Then the last part…That's the part they say that blesses all of nature…asks all of nature and gives thanks. (quoted in Diamond et al. 1994, 31)

Thomas Vennum (1980) has analyzed many archival recordings and notes that Ojibwe song forms were more varied prior to 1910. Still today, there are a few ways in which the standard form may be altered. Drums will sometimes add a coda, or "tail," an extra repetition that may fool the dancers. In addition, if those standing around the drum want to hear an extra repetition, they may whistle as a request to the drum.

The texts of powwow songs are predominantly vocables. This is practical in a tradition with participants who speak dozens of different Native American languages. In some instances, particularly among the Cree, there are lexically meaningful words the singers know. A well-known example is "Darling Don't Cry," a song recorded with vocables by the popular drum Red Bull and then rearranged by Buffy Sainte-Marie. Note that Red Bull as well as Manitoba-born Cree Sainte-Marie, are at home on the prairies, much further west than the nations discussed in this textbook. This song can be legally downloaded from iTunes in the United States, but it is not available from iTunes in Canada, at the time of publication.

ACTIVITY 5.9 *Listen to "Darling Don't Cry." Note the way in which Sainte-Marie uses technology to enhance the voices of the traditional singers and to vary the balance between their voices and hers.*

The powwow drum itself has many symbolically meaningful design elements. It is sometimes said to resemble a European bass drum. Indeed, sometimes bass drums from local marching bands have been used for powwows. But in those cases, the bass drum was "turned"—a concept that is often used to describe how the energy or power of an object might be changed—in order to change its meaning from war to peace. The vertical bass drum became the horizontal powwow drum. Other drums are constructed carefully, or given as gifts to a community. Certain ones have particular songs associated with them, as well as symbolic design elements. The symbolism that I have been taught derives mostly from the Anishnabe drum dance tradition. Anishnabe elder Jim Dumont describes the big drum as a metaphor for a world in itself, or even the lodge of life. The sound goes out in all directions. The drum never rests on the earth, for instance, so that the bottom membrane can resonate. In some areas it is placed on a blanket, held up by the drummers' toes, or suspended from four drum stakes, one at each of the cardinal directions. Sometimes the membranes on top and bottom are given by a male and a female animal to embrace different energies of creation. Sometimes the top membrane is painted, divided in half by a black line separating red and blue semicircles. Some say this line divides good and evil, or night and day, and that drummers walk on both sides of the line. The drum must be treated with respect. Tobacco offerings are often given to honor it.

At certain points in a powwow song, you will hear accented drum strokes known as "honor beats." Dancers respond to these loud beats in various ways, at times by turning toward the drum, at times by raising a handheld feather in a proud gesture. The tempo of the powwow drum always pushes ahead of the beat of the song.

ACTIVITY 5.10   *Listen again to iMix #12, now focusing on the drum. Listen for the accented honor beats. In which phrases of the song form do they occur in this particular song? Add them to the graph you made of this song in a previous activity.*

Women have historically been excluded from sitting around the drum. The explanation for this, however, sometimes surprises non-Native students, since it relates not to any restrictions on women's expressive potential, but rather to the power of their bodies. They have the ability to purify their bodies monthly when they menstruate, a time of the month that may be referred to as their "moon time." Men, on the other hand, do not have this power and must drum to acquire the same spiritual strength. In some communities the prohibition on women touching the drum has been relaxed, but in other places, it is still respected. A role that women do play is to form a circle around the drum, symbolically holding the circle together. They may enter the song an octave above the men at the point in the melody where the opening phrase repeats an octave lower (listen for the women's voices on iMix #16). Sometimes, the men drop out in the final phrase and allow the women to finish the song. This complementarity, in which men start but women finish, men drum but women hold the circle together, is characteristic of many aspects of Anishnabe thinking and has influenced other First Nations in the Northeast.

THE COMMODIFICATION OF POWWOW MUSIC

The earliest commercial recordings of powwow music were those of the singers (and their friends and families) themselves, made at the powwow grounds on boom boxes or other inexpensive cassette recording devices in order to facilitate the learning of new repertoire, or simply to enjoy the songs of another drum. Such early powwow cassettes featured photos of the drum group, sometimes with children and family members. These rather private, family album–style images indicated that the market for the CDs was a local one. Since the late 1980s, however, the packaging of powwow CDs is more varied and the imagery directed at a broader market.

Canyon Records (founded in 1951) and Indian House (established by Tony and Ida Isaacs in 1966) featured some of the earliest commercially available products, with recordings dating back to the early 1950s. Canyon's current catalogue lists hundreds of powwow CDs. Many other companies, as well as independent producers, often the individual drums themselves, are now active. Winnipeg's Sunshine Records is the largest in Canada, but newer companies such as Arbor and Sweet Grass are producing polished recordings that are garnering Native American Music Awards and Canadian Aboriginal Music Awards.

By the turn of the century, some of the most popular Plains groups, such as Black Lodge Singers, Northern Cree, Red Bull, or Whitefish Jrs, had produced upwards of twenty CDs. While these (northern) groups are from western Canada, they are also very popular in provinces further east. The drums that are the most popular shift from year to year and region to region. Sometimes a southern group, such as the Pawnee drum Sizzortail after the release of their first CD, becomes especially popular in Canada for a period of time. Local groups, however, are also well known and loved in their own communities and regions.

The aesthetic of powwow music has subtly shifted in the process of recording. Until the twenty-first century, most commercial recordings of powwow groups were recorded live with one or more microphones placed above the drum and the heads of the singers. Isaacs still favors this means of recording, arguing that the sound is more "natural" if reverberation, synthesizers, or sound effects are added (later) to the original recording. "There are two ways to get Indian music out to the world audience," says Isaacs.

> One way is to modernize the music to make it accessible to people with non-traditional ears. The other way is to encourage people to improve their ears and come over to where the music is. Traditional American Indian music is good just the way it is. It doesn't need to be mixed with anything. For the people who want it, it's here, but they have to make the trip. (www.indianhouse.com)

For those willing to make the trip, Indian House has some exceptional music waiting for them.

In the last few years, companies like Arbor Records have begun to introduce the recording practices of popular music, making overdubs of lead singers, for instance, or recording the drum separately so that the elements can be balanced and manipulated in the postproduction process. Sometimes elements such as the sound of dancers' bells are added in the mix to create sound that is regarded by some as more authentic. Ethnomusicologist Christopher Scales (2004) has studied such mixing effects. His work demonstrates many other examples of the stylistic transformations produced by recording studio practices, and the ways they are linked to the discourses that construct modern Native American identities. This theme will return later in the chapter.

CONTEMPORARY POPULAR MUSIC AND THEATER

Earlier chapters traced the long and intense encounter with Europeans and other "newcomers" along the Atlantic seaboard: in particular, throughout the region sometimes described as the Eastern Woodlands, and more recently, in the northern territories of the Inuit. This colonial encounter both disrupted traditional communities and demanded a capacity for cultural negotiation. Women such as Lucy Nicolar and Santu Toney were among those adept at using varied musical styles as an important part of this process, as described in Chapter 3. This was hardly regionally unique. Native American musicians emphasize that they have always been involved in the production of all genres of North American popular music. Philip Deloria has written about the late nineteenth- and early twentieth-century musical exchanges, emphasizing that music "proved a natural place for cross-cultural meetings" (2004, 205).

> Many had already absorbed tribal musical training and repertoire, at least to some extent, when they first systematically encountered Western music. Music, seen in developmentalist terms, made up a critical part of boarding and day school experience for many Indian children. Bands, orchestras, choruses, and music lessons of all types—these were among the signifiers of civilization. Native students often took up instruments easily, and they brought their musical training with them when they left. (2004, 205)

With reference to the late nineteenth and early twentieth centuries, Deloria discusses the Narragansett composer Thomas Commuck, who was writing in the 1840s; Creek singer Oyapela; Robert Coon, a Lakota sousaphonist in the John Philip Sousa band; Ojibwe tenor Carlisle Kawbawgam, who worked in vaudeville; the Indian String Quartet, Creek singer Tsianina Redfeather; and others. Sam Cronk has written about the baritone Oskenonton (Louie Deer, of Kahnawake, Quebec) and jazz pianist Robert Jamieson, from Six Nations, Ontario (1992, 932).

Turning now to musical media and styles of the late twentieth and early twenty-first centuries, a number of questions arise. Has music continued to mediate "encounter" in the same way? How does it construct modernity for First Nations, Métis, and Inuit people? In what ways is it constrained by the values of other, non-Aboriginal modernities? Does traditional indigenous knowledge play any role in shaping its production, circulation, and reception? Looking at genre, language, themes, style and arrangement, citational practices, and cross-cultural alliances are good ways to begin to answer these questions.

Contemporary Native American musicians who work in a wide range of genres and styles emphasize that they may choose to incorporate traditional sonic elements or not. They do not always need to "wear" their aboriginality, that is, to sound identifiably Native American. Some artists such as Buffy Sainte-Marie and Robbie Robertson, worked in the popular music mainstream early in their careers but acknowledged their First Nations heritage later on. Furthermore, some contemporary Native American music defies mainstream definitions of genres while some fits the industry definitions quite well. Modern indigenous musicians are aware of many different positions within the social spaces and communities of value that different popular music genres imply. What

I mean by "musical communities of value" is that certain types of music become associated with different lifestyles and beliefs. Consider rap and hip-hop, as an example. In the "hood," rap and hip-hop are a music of resistance and witty defiance, but this music and associated lifeways may thrive in many communities remote from the African American ones of the Bronx where it originated. Native American rappers inflect the social shape of the genre to express issues of local importance. Similarly, traces of the concept that the blues is the voice of the oppressed, or that country music has heart and comes from the rural experience of the common man, are still present when artists from new ethnocultural, class-based, urban, and gendered communities begin to create in these styles. But, more importantly, the localization of the style, making it one's own, enables the creation of new meanings and interpretations.

There is another, less positive way to look at the tremendous variety of popular music production in Native America, however. It is less easily distinguished because it uses mainstream genres and is too diverse to be easily identifiable. Hence, when you go to your local music stores, it is hard to predict where you may find Native American CDs. The inconsistency in labeling and classifying contemporary Native American music creates something of a visibility problem.

> **ACTIVITY 5.11** *Go to your local music store and look for recordings of powwow songs, as well as CDs by two or three very well-known Native American recording artists: Buffy Sainte-Marie, Susan Aglukark, Litefoot, Joanne Shenandoah, Walela, or others. Ask the store owner why certain recordings are classified as they are. Be prepared to discuss the pros and cons of the store owner's rationale in your next class.*

This small book does not have sufficient space to permit the exploration of the full range of Native American popular music. I introduce you to nine individual songs or tunes and then compare how they relate to the construction of modern indigenous identity in North America.

> **ACTIVITY 5.12** *Listen to the following nine audio examples: CD tracks 19–26. From your own experience, make notes about the following: genre, language, subject matter of the lyrics, as well as musical style and arrangement. Then study each CD track, guided by my descriptions, to hear additional stylistic features.*

(1) Lee Cremo – "The Mystery Stepdancer" (CD track 19). Mi'kmaq fiddler Lee Cremo (1939-99; Figure 5.7), from Eskasoni, Nova Scotia, is from the earliest generation of musicians represented by these next nine audio examples, a generation that included notable Native American performers such as Peter La Farge, Buffy Sainte-Marie, Morley Loon, Willie Dunn, and Shingoose (Curtis Jonnie). Cremo, who could be considered either Mi'kmaq or Métis, liked to describe his first attempt to play the fiddle as a seven-year old, when the rest of his family had gone to church.

> I took my father's fiddle out from under the bed and thought about how to play it. Of course I had been watching the others, but that's not the same thing as really playing it. I figured out that with four fingers and one thumb on each hand I should be able to figure something out. The first tune I played that morning was "Pop goes the weasel". That was the simplest thing I could think of. It didn't sound that hot either! My notes weren't very good, and my bow arm was kind of scratchy.

FIGURE 5.7 *Lee Cremo (Mi'kmaq) with his grandson.* (Used by permission of the Cremo family)

When they got home from church, my father told me to put the fiddle away and that he would give me some pointers after. He said that this was the day I should be praying too. (interview by Gordon E. Smith, 1990, in Cronk 1990, 60).

Cremo's father, as well as many of the magnificent Cape Breton players of the mid-twentieth century—Winston "Scotty" Fitzgerald, Wilfred Prosper, Dan Hughie MacEachern—and others, such as the Quebecois virtuoso Jean Carignan, taught him well. Cremo became a champion, winning the Maritime Old Time Fiddling Contest six times, an East Coast Music Award, and "Best Bow Arm in the World" at the Grand Master Fiddler Championship in Nashville.

Cremo perfected the Scottish style of Cape Breton (as evident, for instance, in his performance of "Sheehan's Reel" and "Pigeon on the Gate" on Smithsonian Folkways album *Creation's Journey*, which you can legally download from www.folkways.si.edu). Some of his own compositions, however, were arguably influenced by the prevalent use of double-stops and occasional asymmetrical meters or phrase lengths of Métis fiddlers on the Canadian prairies. I say "arguably" because Cremo didn't emphasize his Métis-ness, to my knowledge, preferring to self-identify as Mi'kmaq. Furthermore, recent work on Métis music in eastern Canada challenges earlier prairie-based research accounts by demonstrating that Métis fiddlers are eclectic.

"The Mystery Stepdancer" from his album *The Champion Returns* is, however, a case to consider. The repeated (subdivided) notes at the end of each phrase in this tune use a bowing technique that Cape Breton fiddlers describe as a "cut," but Cremo harmonizes these repeated notes consistently, creating a double-stop sound. The second, higher strain of the tune is longer than the four-square lower strain. These are often regarded as markers of Métis style.

The Cremo family told me that "The Mystery Stepdancer" had a special place in Lee Cremo's heart. "He said he could hear a beat in the background that he couldn't account for in the studio. He wasn't sure who the mystery stepdancer was but we sure had fun discussing spirits and ghosts and stepdancers he could remember from his family and friends, hence the name" (e-mail from Lee's daughter Elizabeth, August 11, 2006).

 (2) Forever – "My Way" (CD track 20). Representing a more recent generation of Mi'kmaq, the Nova Scotian rock band Forever has garnered many regional and national awards, particularly for their second CD, *Something to Dream Of.* Their six-member ensemble includes

the standard roster of vocals, drums, guitars, keyboards, and bass. Most of their songs use the stylistic conventions of mainstream rock, and many voice angst about love or romantic relationships. One might argue, then, that their work does not choose to exhibit Aboriginality at all. They sing in English but enunciate vowels very broadly, in a way that sounds more United States than Canadian. This pronunciation is also represented graphically in the title of the tune "Guitar Thang." Another tune, the flamenco-styled "Sloppy Taco," also contributes to the difficulty of locating the group stylistically and geographically. They choose to look and sound cosmopolitan. One question to ask about their music, then, is whether it matters what the ethnocultural identities of the singers are.

At one level, the song "My Way" reflects the individualism that marks certain stereotypes of masculinity, and the alienation that many young men feel. At another level, however, a listener may think about a different range of issues, knowing it is a Mi'kmaq band singing: "I find it strange everyone / Looks at me and stares." Is this song, after all, about the marginalization of First Nation people? About racism?

Stylistically, the guitar distortion, backbeat percussion patterns, and intense energetic lead singing place this firmly in the rock genre, but there are a couple of less-conventional elements. The form consists of a verse (eight lines), bridge (two lines), and chorus (two lines). Each line of the verse features a descending chromatic line in both the voice and the bass, mostly in unison. The unison is even more prominent in the ascending line of the bridge, perhaps because the rhythms of voice and instruments contrast, making a heterophonic texture. The defiant assertion that "I don't care what people say. / I'm gonna do it my way" is strongly reinforced by this "individualized unison." Is unison a marker of Native American identity after all? Or is it simply a way of emphasizing an important line of text?

Only the chorus is harmonized, both instrumentally and vocally. The back-up vocals are mixed, however, to make them seem somewhat distant. Their strange megaphone-like quality is most noticeable in the break before verse 3, in which the solo voice is left out entirely. One way to read this is to question whether the mix of the back-up vocals sounds alien and unsupportive. Relative to other songs on their CD, this one has more edge, more distortion, and less acoustic warmth.

(3) Trurez Crew – "Why We Rhyme" (CD track 21). The Iroquois group Trurez Crew is part of a huge Native American hip-hop scene. Arguably, rap continues the strong emphasis on the spoken word that characterizes both many types of traditional ceremonialism and

earlier forms of popular music, some of which featured spoken word. John Trudell and Joy Harjo are among the writers whose words were delivered rhythmically with musical accompaniment, beginning in the 1970s. Some work by 7th Fire—a band that included Anishnabe and Caribbean members—was also spoken word, particularly on *Till the Bars Break,* an album they made in the wake of the Oka Crisis in Quebec. By the 1990s, the Native American hip-hop and rap scene included dozens of bands and individual artists: Without Rezervation, TKO, Litefoot, Wayquay, War Party, Eekwol, Shadowyze, and Kinnie Starr, to name only a few of the most prominent. Some made explicit connections to the oppression and marginalization of African Americans. Others, such as Wayquay, included layers of sound that distinctly reference Native American traditional music. While some is "in your face" and aggressive, some Native American rap emphasizes themes of "red pride," and eschews violent or sexist imagery.

Trurez Crew negotiates between quite contrasted messages on their debut album *It's Begun…* They preface their tracks with a bilingual statement read in Cayuga and English on the CD by an elder, after we hear initial calls of "Respect" and "Disrespect." They simultaneously apologize and assert their right to write hard-hitting and, in their words, sometimes offensive lyrics:

> We have been working at this for a long time. We are sorry about the bad things that we say. We don't mean to hurt anyone, especially our own people. We are trying to do something positive with our lives. We are really proud of who we are. Every native person is equally important. We are the original ones and nothing can change that. Now listen… (liner notes)

Their rhymes are "negotiative," at times aggressively applauding a lifestyle with violence, alcohol, and "hos," but at other times more gently articulating a history of oppression and asserting the growing pride of their generation. The four members of the crew, using the names Poppa Cherry, Mojo, Sir Mr Preyemere, and Tha Technician, have distinctive voices and personalities. Tha Technician (Jonathan Lloyd Garlow) rhymes with a Caribbean accent. Most often, their sample-based accompaniments serve as ostinati over which each of the four raps in turn. They use samples of an actor's lines (with a distinct Welsh accent), R & B, movie music, and more classical-sounding keyboard, often featuring the scratchiness of old LPs in the mix. In "Why We Rhyme," the theme of pride is overt as they assert "Red Pride, that's why we rhyme." "*Ongwehonweh*" is rhymed with "Rocks our own way," and the couplet

"It's my duty to make sure this shit is bust / I'll make music from dawn til dusk" becomes a refrain. In the background a piano sample, with a series of broken chords, contrasts in its "politeness" with the rhymes. Close-miked voices contrast with megaphone-like voices mixed to sound distant and alien.

(4) Charlie Panigoniak – "Sweet Tobacco" (CD track 22). From Arviat in Nunavut, the Inuit singer Charlie Panigoniak pioneered the writing of songs in his own language, Inuktitut, long before "world music" was in vogue. He often claims he learned the skill while recovering from tuberculosis in a southern hospital in the early 1970s. His songs bear the traces of English-language folk, country music, and sometimes Christian hymns. Like the Inuk storyteller mentioned in Chapter 1, Charlie loves to use vocal timbres creatively, sometimes creating different voices (for animals, for instance), comic effects, or specific moods. Here he changes his voice to express the satisfaction of smoking tobacco. The repeated word in the refrain of this song is "*mamaaqunit*," a word that can mean "it tastes good," but whose root often refers to an aroma. (The same root is used for the word "perfume," for instance.) Charlie plays with the closed-lip "mmm" as he repeats the melody, adding vocal effects that suggest the pleasure and evoke laughter at the same time. The way he plays with this syllable suggests similar techniques of traditional throat singers, discussed earlier in Chapter 2. Panigoniak often adds extra beats between phrases, just as drum dance singers do when they need to take a breath. In these ways, his songs meld practices from tradition with genres of music learned in modern institutions or from contemporary media.

Unlike the band Forever, whose lyrics might be interpreted as either thematically mainstream or First Nations–related, Panigoniak's lyrics are unquestionably about his own experience and his life in the north. He uses his own language and has produced most of his recordings in conjunction with public broadcasting in the north (the Canadian Broadcasting Company's Northern Service) rather than seeking a bigger profile with commercial audio recording companies.

Panigoniak's work contrasts in many ways with that of Susan Aglu-kark, the Inuit musician who has come closest to superstardom thus far. She has been affiliated with EMI since the second of her six albums to date, has had chart-topping hits, and has performed before dignitaries in many countries. While her gentle, clear voice produces well as a pop singer, her songs and choices of language often reveal her distinctiveness. For instance, she sings most often in English but includes Inuktitut lyrics in some songs, and non-Inukitut vocables in others. For the most part, she sings her own compositions, often cowritten with her producer Chad Irshik, but there are some well-known tunes, such as "Amazing Grace," in Inuktitut on early albums.

A Pentacostal minister's daughter who grew up in Arviat, Nunavut, Aglukark is not afraid to overlay her music with Christian references, as in the song "Kathy I," or inspirational messages, as in "Stand Up" (available on iTunes). While many of her songs are positive in spirit, she addresses some emotionally challenging subject matter, including suicide in the north, old age, and the victims of war. While Panigoniak's audience is largely a northern Inuktitut-speaking one, Aglukark's varies from one song to the next, but she clearly intends to reach beyond the local with her music.

The imagery on her CD covers, as well as her sound itself, is at times filled with Inuit references (the song "This Child" has an "*aja*" chorus, for instance), and at other times filled with more generalized indigenous markers (vocables that do not relate to Inuit musical practices, or frame drum sounds that are quite unlike the Inuit deep-sounding q*ilaut*). Hence, while Panigoniak's music is solidly grounded in local experience, Aglukark's ranges in different directions.

ACTIVITY 5.13   *Compare the balance and spatial placement of Panigoniak's voice on CD track 20 with Aglukark's in the song "Stand Up" (iMix #17).*

(5) Kashtin – "Akua Tuta" (iMix #18).   The Innu duo Kashtin ("tornado"), originally from Maliotenam, Quebec, consists of Florent Vollant and Claude McKenzie. They made history in Canada in the 1990s when their three commercial albums, all in their language, Innu-aimun (a language spoken by about 10,000), went platinum. In Canada, this means they sold over 200,000 copies. This was a group, then, that had an impact far beyond its own community and even its own nation, since it also received airtime in the United States and Europe, particularly in France, where one song became number one on the pop charts. The two musicians are still on the scene, although each is now working as a solo act. Because there was so much media as well as academic attention to their work of the 1990s, however, we have many perspectives on Kashtin's positioning within the popular music worlds. We can begin to interpret the many values, associations, and meanings that listeners assigned to their work.

Kashtin was by no means the first Innu group to write contemporary pop songs in the artists' own language. A pioneer was Philippe McKenzie, whose work was recorded by Radio Canada (the French-language division of the Canadian Broadcasting Corporation) in the 1980s. Furthermore, there had been earlier contemporary songs, including "*Uishama*," a song composed by Claude's grandfather, Alexandre McKenzie III, as a welcoming song for young women. "*Uishama*" was recorded by Kashtin on their album *Innu* (1994). In other words, the line between traditional *nikamuna* and contemporary compositions had been bridged decades earlier.

The connection of contemporary Innu popular music to tradition was further emphasized in the 1980s by the occasional use of the *teuei-kan*, the frame drum of hunters described in Chapter 3. Sometimes the snare that resonated "spirit voices" was removed for the performance of pop songs. The *teueikan* was never used by Kashtin on their recordings, however. In live performance, Kashtin also dared to feature whistling in many of their early songs. Many Native American groups have strong beliefs about whistling, and the Innu are no exception. Innu elders explain that the northern lights that dance in the sky in cold weather may come down and snatch up someone who whistles. By the time they began making commercial recordings, Kashtin eliminated the whistling, but used vocables for many of the same melodic lines.

In the mid-1980s, Kashtin tried out a new genre label for their songs, "folk Innu," but genre creation is a complex matter. The music industry prefers a relatively fixed number of genre labels around which it can organize markets, so attempts to label something in a new way are often precarious. The "folk Innu" label was not retained once Kashtin brought out their first recording.

Kashtin's songs are often about relationships, but in a much more inclusive way than mainstream pop: among generations, between human and four-legged creatures, in relation to places. Romantic love songs are rare in Innu songwriting. Among their hits are titles such as "*Tshinuau*" ("All of You"), "*Nuitsheiuan*" ("My Friend"), or "*Uas-set*" ("The Children"). Arguably, this inclusive way of writing about relationships contributes to the strong sense of community that they engender.

The most memorable performance by Kashtin (Figure 5.8) that I ever heard was at a festival called "Innu Nikamu" ("The Indian Sings" or "Songs of the Indian") in the late 1980s, an annual event founded by Florent Vollant that still attracts thousands of First Nations, Inuit, and Métis performers and fans to the remote community of Maliotenam

FIGURE 5.8   *Kashtin (Innu) performing at Innu Nikamu in the late 1980s.*   *(Photo by B. Diamond)*

near Sept-Iles, Quebec. The local stars were back home. When they sang *"Tshinanu"* ("What We Are") in the wee hours of the morning at the end of a long concert, the audience wouldn't let them stop. Their fans sang the difficult rhythms and catchy vocables of the chorus over and over. Sociologists Grenier and Morrison have argued that the use of a vocable refrain allows the audience an "affective link" to the music (in Straw et al. 1995, 129). If I ever needed a demonstration that a single song could inspire people to feel as one, that event was convincing. It is no wonder that this song is sometimes called the Innu national anthem.

Another of their hit songs is *"Akua Tuta"* (available on our iMix #18), the title track of their third CD; the song was also licensed for the TV show *Due South*. The words advise us to care for ourselves, protect the earth, and remember where we are from. "If I'm no longer a child of the Earth, I no longer know where I come from. I no longer recognize my brothers," they sing. Like many of their other songs, the primary harmonies, short phrases, and form are easy to learn. This one has a simpler vocable refrain than most—just *"He, he, he, he."* More complex are the metric asymmetries, or the slightly unusual way the words are spaced within a phrase (as with the phrase *"Akua tuta"*). Florent Vollant relates these asymmetries to the rhythms of the Innu-aimun language.

The short phrases with at least half of the phrase "empty" remind me of the pacing of Innu storytellers, who pause after each phrase to wait for listeners' response.

Kashtin's music, however, cannot be regarded in isolation from other popular-music developments in Quebec in the 1980s and 1990s, as sociologists Grenier and Morrison have demonstrated. Kashtin were popular at the period of intense Quebec nationalism leading up to a narrowly defeated referendum on independence. While Kashtin preferred not to take a public stand on the issue of Quebec sovereignty, they were often used as the face and voice of difference in Quebec, to counter those who argued that the Francophone majority was not sympathetic to cultural diversity. Grenier and Morrison write:

> Kashtin's success represents the first time, not only that a local group who sing in a language other than French has enjoyed so much popularity within the Quebec milieu, but moreover, that an artist or group who sing in another language has been accepted as specifically indigenous, that is, *Québecois*. (In Straw, et al. 1995, 127)

They point to the fact that the Innu are one of the few First Nations in Quebec who speak French as a second language, and to the parallels between the battle to maintain Aboriginal language and culture in relation to the struggle of Francophones in Canada. They also note that Kashtin's success in France has cultural currency in Canada.

(6) Murray Porter – "1492 Who Found Who" (CD track 23).   Many have asked why some genres, particularly the blues, have resonated so strongly in Native American communities. Musicians such as Ulali are raising questions about the possible contributions that Native Americans in the American South have made to the development of the blues. In the North and East, particularly in communities along the Canada–United States border, the genre was readily heard on the radio from Buffalo, Detroit, and Chicago, and became immensely popular. The local radio station at Six Nations has broadcast many hours of blues for decades; a nationwide TV series called *Rez Bluez* is masterminded by Elaine Bomberry, from this same community. As with rap, there is, arguably, an identification with the common forms of oppression of Native and African Americans, but also an aesthetic that values the resignification of the familiar. As the lyrics of his song "*1492. Who Found Who?*" assert, Murray Porter likes to describe himself as a "red man who sings a black man's blues in a white man's world."

With friends, some of whom eventually formed his current group, the Pappy Johns Band, Murray Porter (Figure 5.9) has been playing in the Six Nations community for over twenty-five years. Porter's debut album, featuring his own songs, was *1492 Who Found Who* (1994), on the First Nations Music label.

The title track from that 1994 album (CD track 23) offers a new and humorous perspective on "Old Chris Columbus." It is lighthearted until perhaps the intense growl of Porter's voice intensifies the line "How can you find what was not lost?" On the Nashville-recorded CD, a rich arrangement, with interspersed horn riffs, back-up female vocals, and a soulful harmonica solo (played by an unidentified sideman), complements Porter's distinctive voice. An earlier cassette, released under the same album name but recorded at Grant Avenue Studio in Hamilton, has only a few of the same songs and in quite different arrangements. The earlier version of "1492 Who Found Who?" has no brass or female back-up singers. It represents an example of the difference between a locally oriented (and modestly budgeted) and an internationally oriented recording.

(7) Ulali — "Museum Cases" (CD track 24). The trio Ulali was introduced in Chapter 4. The extraordinary stylistic range of Pura Fe, Soni Moreno, and Jennifer Kreisberg, their virtuosic vocal abilities, and their powerful songs captured not only a fan base but the imaginations of mainstream pop artists such as the Indigo Girls and movie producers

FIGURE 5.9   *Murray Porter.*   *(Photo courtesy of Elaine Bomberry and Murray Porter)*

such as Sherman Alexie. Like the music of other contemporary Native American artists, their music is often playful, sometimes soulful, occasionally nostalgic. We heard several of their rattle songs earlier (CD track 18). Unlike those, "Museum Cases" is one of a small group of their songs that is overtly political.

Pura Fe described the genesis of this song:

> Well, actually it started out 'cause I used to stay in Arizona a lot with a good friend of mine. He does a lot of work for the treaty council. So I travelled with him on a couple of trips and saw things. And one journey started at Wounded Knee during the memorial. You know, you take that in. And after that, we drove to Minneapolis and we went into the women's prison, the Indian program, and you take that in. And we ended up in Boston at the Peabody ... [My friend] was checking up on some remains and things that were taken ... So, we met with the director of the Peabody Museum. He wouldn't even meet us in his office; he met us in the hallway. So I took that in. So, it wasn't till I got home that it all registered. The way we exist and the everyday struggles ... So yeah, it's important that we talk about our [experiences]. The fact that we're able to have a microphone, the fact that we're able to travel, the fact that we have a voice, it's very important we say everything we can say about our people, our communities, our home, and everything, to preserve ourselves. (interview with author, 2000)

While one might describe "Museum Cases" as a protest song, Pura Fe's comments are not framed in political terms. You "take that in," she says. She reflects on personal experience in this moving critique of the collections of archaeological remains in museums. Ulali is not concerned here about NAGPRA (the Native American Graves Protection and Repatriation Act), the American legislation that governs repatriation, but with the psychological impact of such immense disrespect. They sing in English—the only practical language for subject matter that critiques "encounter"—with slight southern inflections in pronunciation and vocal display.

The song starts with the most daring of musical gestures, an extended unison section without a regular metric structure. It's a good choice for a seemingly factual account: "I was looking at myself buried alive." Ulali shift from song to speech to talk about "government research, science, churches." There are moments of stasis. The triadic patterns on "Take you still" are musically stabilizing, but what do those words mean? Do they ask whether "you still take"? To my ears, the triadic ostinato implies mainstream complacency, as Ulali sing "Sterilized women cannot give birth." The song intensifies with the enormous slide up to the word "Exploitation," and crests at the phrase "How can money justify the greed?" But the real climax is an ironically gentle phrase with sweet triadic harmonies on "genocide." The line "No guilt, no shame" recurs several times in the song, always effecting a shift in the rhythm, and finally it is uttered gently at the end.

While this is the most overtly political of the songs selected for comment in this chapter, it is important to observe that Native American musicians should never be viewed as always and only political. Ulali sing about lost love, about Grandpa's banjo, or about Mother Earth. As individual performers, their repertoires are eclectic in still other ways. But perhaps unlike nonindigenous performers, they feel they must, as Pura Fe so eloquently argued, speak out about the experiences they have had.

(8) Joy Harjo – "A Post Colonial Tale" (CD track 25). Harjo, widely known as a distinguished poet and writer, is a Muscogee (Creek) originally from the Southeast but now a resident of Hawaii. Like many contemporary artists, then, she is a cosmopolitan whose life cannot be located in a single place. Her artistic talents are multiple: she sings, plays saxophone, and also does visual art. She conceives of her poetry as an oral art, and, for that reason, she has produced CDs that have become increasingly complex in their sonic layering. With her band, Poetic Justice, she evokes and invokes powwow-based music, jazz, and reggae, in a mix that defies genre definitions. She describes the hybridity of her sound as follows:

> The music that speaks for us is a blend of influences that speak of community, love for people, for all creatures, for this crazy beautiful history and the need to sing with and of the sacred. These musics are our respective tribal musics, from Muscogee, Northern Plains, Hopi to Navajo; reggae, a music born of the indomitable spirit of a tribal people in a colonized land; jazz, a music born of the need to sing by African peoples in this country, a revolutionary movement of predominately African sources influenced by European and the southern tribes; and rock and blues, musics cradled in the south that speak of our need to move with heart and soul through this land, this spiral of life. We are forged by this dance for justice and the absolute need to sing." (liner notes, 1997)

In "A Postcolonial Tale," from her 1997 album *Letter from the End of the Twentieth Century,* she frames the narration with powwow singing with the big drum and bells. The soprano saxophone (played by Harjo) enters after the phrase "This is the first world, and the last," and returns with reference to the "imagination." Her sound bends pitches, like it is struggling to become. In between, her recitation is underpinned by skank guitar (offbeat figures played by rhythm guitar and sometimes also piano in reggae), bass, and drums. The vocal rhythms and accents in the accompaniment coincide heavily on key words such as "guns" in the phrase "The children were in school learning subtraction with guns," or playfully trade upbeat syncopations on the phrase "of rising up." For Harjo, then, music enhances and carries the message, and the message embraces all humanity, not just Native American society.

(9) BONES: An Aboriginal Dance Opera (produced and directed by Sadie Buck) (CD track 26).   In the final example, we will consider how a mainstream genre from European classical tradition has been redefined in the hands of Sadie Buck and David DeLeary. Produced in 2001 at the Banff Centre for the Arts, where Sadie Buck had directed the Aboriginal Women's Voices program for five years and Alejandro Ronceria had led the Chinook Winds Aboriginal Dance Program, the work *BONES* (Figure 5.10) was billed as "An Aboriginal Dance Opera." Reinstating the unity of song and dance was one of the objectives of the codirectors. They describe their vision as follows:

> We have also set forth on a path that is new. We are pioneering a new idea with this performance. The cast and crew are primarily Indigenous, and many of our people have dreamed of working on a major production where the ideology and story is Indigenous and where the cast and crew are Indigenous…

> The story of *BONES* is the life of a people… We love the land we were placed in. We work to keep our lands safe and healthy. We are sovereign in our hearts and our minds. We try our best to work in harmony with the earth, the sustainer of our life. Our memory, *BONES* is about our life. *BONES* is about our love, our peace, our existence. (from the directors' statement in the *BONES* program)

In order to create a work that was "for all the people of the earth," the codirectors created a new language, one they called the "Language of the World" because it borrowed elements from many different languages. The music is also syncretic, with elements of various indigenous musics, electronica, and popular music. The staging of the work often depicted an earthly realm (lower level) and a spirit realm (upper level). The concept is premised on the idea that the earth is composed of bones, the remnants of life on its surface. The themes of birth, knowledge, survival, the game, grandmother (i.e., aging), and dying are enacted in act 1. Act 2 focuses on community, on fractures/silence, and

FIGURE 5.10   *Scene from the Aboriginal Dance Opera* BONES.   *(Courtesy of Donald Lee, photographer, and the Banff Centre for the Arts)*

on the seven brothers (common to many indigenous mythologies) who re-created life. Act 3 returns to themes of birth, life ("Sea Shells"), and death ("Ashes and Ashes").

Two short excerpts comprise CD track 26. The first accompanies a stylized Native American Bone Game (read again the reference to dice bowl games in Chapter 3), but the chant is reminiscent of Maori *hakka*, a vigorous traditional dance often related to preparation for battle. The second excerpt is a chorale-like piece that is performed in two scenes entitled "Mother-Child."

> **ACTIVITY 5.14**   *Choose one of the following elements: language and accent, lyric themes, musical arrangement, production values (mixing techniques), cross-cultural citation, or collaboration. Listen again to the previous nine examples, focusing on the element you have chosen, and noting what you hear. Write an essay about that element in relation to the previous nine examples of Native American popular music and theater.*

CONTEMPORARY NATIVE AMERICAN MUSIC AND IDENTITY

The examples above have barely scratched the tip of an iceberg of contemporary Native American music. Of what are they representative? No single thing, I hope. They were not chosen because they are virtuosic, or radical, or authoritative, or political, or catchy, although some of them are some of those things. The songs and tunes discussed here are performed by good indigenous musicans making music in a variety of ways. Even with these few examples, very different approaches can be seen to language and dialect choice, to genre definition, to the subject matter of lyrics, to style and arrangement, and to musical alliances among and beyond the First Nations, Inuit, or Métis communities. In the music of each artist, these choices work together to construct modern indigenous identities, to encounter new audiences, and at times also to try to remain true to certain traditional values.

As Berger and Carroll (2003) and other ethnomusicologists have demonstrated, globalization has made the matter of language and dialect choice a crucial identity issue. In relation to the imminent disappearance of a language, the currency it has in the modern world, or the alliances that a particular dialect or accent might signify, the way one speaks and sings is loaded with signification. Aboriginal musicians must decide whether to perform in English in order to reach a wider audience, or to use their native language to reflect on political, intellectual, or social issues from a culturally specific perspective. They must decide whether to pronounce words in such a way that their community, region, ethnicity, or nation is identified or whether to sound cosmopolitan. Their choice of language, dialect, or accent may also indicate an alliance with an American, African American, Canadian, or other audience. They must be aware of their listeners' perceptions of class, relating to vocabulary and dialect. Each decision has implications. Hence, Forever chooses not to locate themselves. They write in Canadian English but utter words in a "United States" way. They create songs that could be interpreted as First Nations–related, or not. Joy Harjo similarly uses English, but the hybrid stylistic references in her music emphasize difference and solidarity at the same time. Kashtin and Charlie Panigoniak, on the other hand, choose to remain close to their communities by writing in their first languages and by reflecting themes and issues that stem from their community-based experience. There are implications to each choice.

Genre definition is similarly a complex matter. The experience of Kashtin demonstrates that naming a new genre is a risky strategy that challenges industry norms. Music, like that of Ulali or Harjo, may defy simple genre categories, or it may appropriate and change a genre category as the opera *BONES* does. The choice of a genre such as rap or blues may imply an actual or symbolic alliance with the positionality of African Americans, or may simply be a product of the mediated listening experience of a specific generation, as it was for Murray Porter. Many Native Americans both excel in the performance of mainstream genres and subtly challenge the styles and structures of those genres in some of their own compositions, as Lee Cremo has done.

Decisions about style and arrangement often involve teams of collaborators. Hence, it is not always clear who makes the choices about these matters, as with Murray Porter when he rerecorded in Nashville, or Susan Aglukark, who cowrites and arranges with sidemen from a variety of musical worlds. The position of an artist may also be influenced by nonindigenous issues, as in the case of Kashtin, whose music was produced within a social scene charged with the idealism of Quebecois sovereignists. On the other hand, style can reflect cross-cultural alliances, the exigencies of textual expression, or personal aesthetic preferences. In instances where the citation of a contrasting style is the norm, as with hip-hop, the listeners' associations with the sampled style are an important dimension of the message—in the work of Trurez Crew, for instance.

These are the elements of what Gerald Vizenor (1994) has called being "post Indian." The position of contemporary indigenous musicians is like that of all contemporary musicians who must negotiate the nuances of language, genre, and style. What is different is the history and the social themes that are of importance to them as individuals and community members, the range of languages that inform their songwriting practices, the varied traditional musics of their people that most are keenly aware of, and their clear vision that they speak as modern Aboriginal people.

Epilogue

∞

This textbook explores First Nations and Inuit musical traditions in the northern and eastern parts of North America. The specific traditions discussed in this book were carefully chosen with advice from a team of Inuit and First Nations advisors. While reference has been made to the rich ceremonial life of the nations and communities discussed, we have selected song traditions that are widely shared with nonindigenous people for the most extensive discussion. As Sadie Buck observes, the sharing of these traditions is intended to celebrate the gifts of Creation, the gifts that sustain life.

The themes of traditional knowledge, encounter, and modernity were woven through each of the chapters. To approach these themes, I assumed, *a priori,* that no history of Native America can be created without the recognition that five hundred years of cohabitation between indigenous people and newcomers is a central formative factor. Colonialism has a lot to answer for. Indigenous communities were relocated with tragic loss of life and equally tragic loss of community and land-based knowledge systems. Missionization was often not respectful of indigenous ceremonies and beliefs. Social inequities were perpetuated by racist institutions. The history, however, is far from a simple picture of victimization. As we have seen, Native Americans found ways to perpetuate their traditions, to adapt those of the "visitors" to their lands, to safeguard the values and at least some of the languages that sustained them, and to find ways to laugh through life's challenges.

It is clear that music and dance traditions played a vital role in these processes. Traditional styles of music are often very good means of commenting on new encounters. Traditional singers find ways to mirror new elements in their worlds—as Inuit throat singers do, for instance. At times singers use traditional forms to comment on the effects of new machines or institutions—as the *Ęhsgá:nye:* singers who joke about bingo do. At other times, the song mediates the encounter itself, as with Mi'kmaq welcoming songs.

It is equally clear that Native American musicians have been adept at learning new styles of music and adapting them for their purposes. Such was the "artful activism" of nineteenth-century vaudevillians such as Lucy Nicolar and Molly Spotted Elk, as well as contemporary popular music artists such as Ulali, Joy Harjo, or Trurez Crew.

While this book articulates my assumption that traditions of knowledge and ways of knowing are often rooted differently, it argues that these roots continue to shape the many modernities of the late twentieth and early twenty-first centuries. That is, traditional knowledge and modern knowledge are not presented as dichotomous and separate realms. The former—rooted in ways of observing the natural and social worlds, rooted in concepts about how individuals and groups might best be sustained—feeds and is interwoven with the latter.

Music is a means by which this interweaving takes place. Cowboy songs may influence Haudenosaunee social dance songs. Opera may be transformed by the fusion of traditional with modern song and dance in the hands of an indigenous artist. The technologies of the recording studio may both change traditional aesthetics, as they have in the case of powwow music, and be rethought because of tradition. As Deloria observes, "The sound of Indian continues to lurk along the ridge tops and in the deserts of our cultural memory, a couple of pounding chords, or a snippet of melody" (2004, 222). While music relates to expectations about Native Americans, these modern traditions often disrupt the easy stereotypes that have been so pervasive in schools and society in general. By continuing to make music of many different kinds, First Nations, Inuit, and Métis people are finding a powerful place in the global community of the twenty-first century.

Glossary

A'tukan (Mi'kmaq) classic story or legend; information that has always been around; cf. *atnuhan* (Innu), story or legend

Agnutmakan (Mi'kmaq) news, recent information

Ajaja an Inuit drum dance song; see also *pisiq*

Aqausiq (Inuit) short song of affection made for a child or other family member

Atǫ:wí:sę: (Haudenosaunee) women's planting song, characterized by its high vocal tessitura

Crow Hop a powwow dance, characterized by a hopping step that mimics the movement of a crow

Drum can refer to various types of membranophone; may also refer to the singing group associated with a specific powwow drum

Duck Dance a social dance of the Haudenosaunee people in which pairs of women and men move in opposite directions within the circle; when they meet, the men form an arch and the women pass under it until the men capture one pair of women. Other nations, such as the Anishnabe, also have a Duck Dance with related choreography

Earth songs a more accurate designation by the Haudenosaunee for genres that are sometimes called "social dance songs"

Ęhsga:nye: (Haudenosaunee) a song-dance genre sometimes called the Women's Shuffle Dance; women move counterclockwise around the dance circle using a close-to-the-ground twisting step

Fancy Dance a category of competition dance in the powwow; regalia includes a colorful double bustle and a wide variety of reflective materials; dance includes acrobatic spins and knee bends; dance tempo for the Men's Fancy Dance is generally the fastest of powwow dances

Gadā:tro:t a Haudenosaunee social dance of the stomp dance type, also called the Standing Quiver Dance

Gaihwi:yo: (Haudenosaunee) literally "good news," a reference to the teachings (sometimes called the "Code") of Handsome Lake

Ganǫhǫnyǫhk (Haudenosaunee) the "Thanksgiving Address"; a formally patterned speech that generally opens both social and ceremonial events

Giveaway part of the general emphasis among Native American people on gift giving, a "giveaway" may refer to a powwow event at which gifts are given to those who contribute to the event, sometimes including virtually all attendees

Gourd Dance a southern Plains men's dance originating with the Kiowa; originally associated with the Gourd Clan, it has developed into an intertribal dance that was incorporated into the powwow in certain areas

Great Feather Dance a ceremonial dance that is part of the midwinter cycle of the Haudenosaunee

Great Law of Peace a series of teachings that were brought to the Haudenosaunee nation by a man generally known as the Peacekeeper, between the eleventh and fifteenth centuries

Green Corn Ceremonies while most Eastern Woodlands nations have a ceremonial complex known as Green Corn, the forms are very different in the Northeast and Southeast; for the Haudenosaunee, the ceremony is part of a larger annual cycle of Longhouse "doings," many of which are tied to agriculture; for the Eastern Cherokee or Seminole, the ceremony is an annual form of renewal, involving dance, feasting, a ritualized ballgame, the drinking of emetics or other forms of purification, and other religious observances

Handsome Lake a Haudenosaunee visionary whose severe illness at the turn of the nineteenth century gave rise to teachings that formed the basis of the contemporary Longhouse religion

Hethuska a warrior society of the Ponca, Kansa and Omaha, the songs and dances of which, generally referred to as "war dances," are one of the main sources of contemporary powwow practices

Hoop Dance a Plains "show" dance that is sometimes performed at intertribal events throughout North America: the dancer creates a set of images (flowers, butterflies, eagle, earth, and others that are sometimes described as a renewal of Creation) with a set of twenty-eight hoops that he or she manipulates while dancing continuously

Incomplete repetition form a term used by ethnomusicologists to describe song forms such as that of the powwow in which the group repeats part but not all of the song phrases: A (solo) A (group)| |:BCD:| |

Inuit Qaujimajatuqangit Inuit traditional knowledge, a concept adopted by the Nunavut government in Canada's eastern Arctic

Ji'kmaqn (Mi'kmaq) a shaker or rattle made by splitting an ash strip into thin layers along about half its length; played by hitting the split segment against the hand

Jingle Dress Dance the newest type of powwow competition dance for women, involving an outfit that has small metal cones sewn on it; often said to originate in an Anishnabe medicine society in Ontario

Katajjaq **(pl.** *katajjait*) (Inuktitut) a label used in Nunavik (northern Quebec) for the vocal games often called throat singing; see also *pirqusirtuq*

Kisu'lk (Mi'kmaq) the creation story of the Mi'kmaq people

Kluskap (Mi'kmaq) a popular culture hero in the Mi'kmaq creation story

Ko'jua (Mi'kmaq) a fast-tempo social dance song genre

Longhouse (Haudenosaunee) the traditional style of communal housing (prior to and in the early colonial period) with a shared central fire; now the equivalent to a church, the building where ceremonies of the Longhouse religion are conducted

Makushan (Innu) community feasts involving dance to the accompaniment of the *teueikan*

Mawiomi (Mi'kmaq) a generic word for gathering, now applied to a range of events, including contemporary gatherings and powwows

Medeolinuwok (Wolastoqiyik Peskotomuhkatiyik) medicine person

Nikamun (Innu Cree) generic term for song but generally reserved for songs received in dreams; compare other Algonquian language variants such as the Anishnabe *nagamon* or *nakamun*

Ogweho:weh (Haudenosaunee) real people; variant Ongwehonwe

Omaha Dance also called the Grass Dance with reference to braids of sweetgrass worn as part of the regalia, the Omaha Dance was the name given to the War Dance by Northern Plains tribes in the late nineteenth century

Partridge Dance a social dance type for many Wabenaki people; sometimes performed to a *ko'jua*-type song by the Mi'kmaq

Peach Stone Game originating in the Haudenosaunee creation story, this is a ceremonial event within the midwinter ceremonies

Pictographs images incised or painted on stone

Pine Cone Dance a women's dance genre of several First Nations of the Wabenaki Confederacy

Pirqusirtuq (Inuktitut) a label for the women's vocal games generally called throat singing in parts of Nunavut (see also *katajjaq*)

Pisiq (**pl**. *pisiit*) (Inuktitut) drum dance song in most regions of Nunavut and the Northwest Territories

Powwow thought to be a Narragansett (eastern Algonquian) word for a medicine ceremony; subsequently used to name an intertribal gathering featuring singing, feasting, and social dancing

Puamun (**pl**. *puamuna*) (Innu) dream

Push-up In reference to powwow songs, it indicates a complete repetition of the song melody (analogous to a complete strophe)

Qaggi (Inuit) traditional communal "house," often a large iglu with family alcoves around the perimeter; drum dancing was one activity that took place in this space

Qilaut (Inuktitut) the name of the large frame drum with wooden handle that is turned from side to side and struck on the wooden frame edges with a thick wooden stick; accompanies Inuit drum dance songs

Rabbit Dance a social dance genre, performed by couples, brought to the Haudenosaunee from Oklahoma. A male and female partner cross hands so that their left hands are joined and their right hands; they take two steps forward and one back

Robin Dance a Haudenosaunee social dance genre celebrating the return of the robin in the spring

Round Dance a social dance genre that many First Nations share, often used to welcome all participants

Sanguagusiit (Inuit) name for the transitions between patterns in Inuit vocal games (throat songs)

Shaking Tent Ceremony a ceremony of many Eastern Algonquian nations (including the Innu) in which a medicine person communicates with the animal masters and other spirits in a small tent structure

Shawl Dance a powwow dance type for girls and women also known as the Women's Fancy Dance, in which a colorful fringed shawl is worn around the shoulders and manipulated in the course of the dance; the movement resembles the fluttering of the butterfly

Shell-shakers senior women in the Southeast who wear turtle-shell rattles (or, more recently, tin-can shakers) on their legs in the stomp dance

Sing In the context of a Haudenosaunee community, it refers to a biannual intercommunity event at which old and new *Ęhsga:nye:* (Women's Shuffle Dance songs) are performed

Smoke Dance a rapid social dance of the Haudenosaunee, now often included in powwows of the Northeast

Snake Dance 1) a Wabenaki dance that symbolizes the coiling and exuviation of the snake; 2) a social dance for all participants at a powwow involving a single line of dancers who weave through the powwow space

Sneak-Up Dance a powwow noncompetitive dance type in which the dancer mimics the stalking of an animal while the drum shifts rhythms from a rapid tremolo to a steady dance pulse

Spectrograph a computer-generated, graphic display of the acoustic information (overtones, intensity, durations) of a segment of sound

Standing Quiver Dance a type of Haudenosaunee stomp dance used to open a social (see *Gadā:tro:t*)

Stomp Dance (Southeast) a socioceremonial event of Woodlands nations (including those who relocated to Oklahoma) involving antiphonal song and accompaniment by women who dance with leg rattles made from turtle shells or tin cans

Stomp Dance (Haudenosaunee) a social dance involving antiphonal song but no accompaniment

TIK an abbreviation developed in the late twentieth century for "traditional indigenous knowledge"; closely related to TEK ("traditional ecological knowledge")

Teueikan (Innu) frame drum, generally suspended for performance, in which a rim and sinew lacing hold the membrane and one or sometimes two snares (with small bone or wood pieces as rattlers); drummer holds the drum by a loop at the base and beats in either a tremolo or triple (short-long) pattern; used as a tool to reconnect with one's dream

Throat singing the common English-language label for the vocal games of Inuit women. It involves a close exchange of short motifs and vocal sounds that often imitate environmental sounds

Tipatshimun (Innu) stories, including more recent narratives and news, in contrast with the classic legends known as *atnuhana*

Trading song genre designation for a type of song common among communities of the Wabenaki Confederacy

Turtle Island North America, in Haudenosaunee legends; now commonly referenced by other First Nations

Waltes (Mi'kmaq) a game played with marked bones or small wooden discs

Wampum small beads of white shell (from several mollusks) and purple shell (from the quahog clam), made into strings or belts with images that recorded and symbolized social or political agreements or alliances; used in treaty negotiations, the beads were also regarded by colonizers as currency

War dance song repertoire associated with the warrior societies of several Plains nations that became central to the development of the powwow

Water drum a small membrane-covered keg drum, partially filled with water; the variant described in this book is the handheld Haudenosaunee water drum, in which the taut, wet membrane has a distinctive high pitch when struck with the delicate stick. Together with cow-horn shakers, the water drum is the main accompaniment for Haudenosaunee social dance songs

References

Alstrup, Kevin. 2004. "Mi'kmaq Atukwaqann and Aural Symbolism in the Music-Making of Thomas George Poulette." In *Papers of the 35th Algonquian Conference,* edited by H.C. Wolfart, 1–12. Winnipeg: University of Winnipeg Press.

Armitage, Peter. 1992. "Religious Ideology Among the Innu of Eastern Quebec and Labrador." *Religiologiques* 6: 64–110. Online at www.unites.uqam.ca/religiologiques/no6/armit.pdf.

Arnakak, Jaypeetee. 2000. "What is Inuit Qaujimajatuqangi?" *Nunatsiaq News,* August 25, 2000. Online at www.nunatsiaq.com.

Augustine, Stephen. 2005. "Silas T. Rand's Work among the Mi'kmaq." Paper presented at the Aboriginal Oral Traditions conference, Gorsebrook Institute, St. Mary's University, Halifax.

Basso, Keith. 1996. "Wisdom Sits in Places: Notes on a Western Apache Landscape." In *Senses of Place,* edited by Steven Feld and Keith Basso, 53–90. Santa Fe: School of American Research Press.

Battiste, Marie. 1997. "Mi'kmaq Socialization Patterns." In *Anthology of Mi'kmaq Writers,* edited by L. Choyce and R. Joe, 145–161. East Lawrencetown, NS: Pottersfield Press.

Battiste, Marie, and James (Sa'ke'j) Youngblood Henderson. 2000. *Protecting Indigenous Knowledge and Heritage: A Global Challenge.* Saskatoon: Purich.

Battiste, Marie. 2000. *Reclaiming Indigenous Voice and Vision.* Vancouver: UBC Press.

Beaudry, Nicole, and Claude Charron. 1978. "Towards Transcription and Analysis of Inuit Throat Games." *Ethnomusicology* 22/2:245–259.

Berger, Harris, and M. T. Carroll, eds. 2003. *Global Pop. Local Language.* Jackson: University of Mississippi Press.

Bigenno, Michelle. 2002. *Sounding Indigenous: Authenticity in Bolivian Music Performance.* New York: Palgrave.

Browner, Tara. 2002. *Heartbeat of the People: Music and Dance of the Northern Pow–wow.* Urbana: University of Illinois Press.

Cavanagh, Beverley. 1982. *Music of the Netsilik Eskimo: A Study of Stability and Change.* Ottawa: National Museums.

Champagne, Duane. 1998. "American Indian Studies is for Everyone." In *Natives and Academics,* edited by Devon A. Mihesuah, 181–189. Lincoln: University of Nebraska Press.

Cronk, M. Sam. 1988. "Writing While They're Singing: A Conversation about Longhouse Social Dance Songs." *New York Folklore* 14/3–4:49–60.

Cronk, M. Sam. 1992. "Non-traditional music." In "Native North Americans in Canada" in *Encyclopedia of Music in Canada,* 2nd edition, edited by H. Kallmann, et al., 931–933. Toronto: University of Toronto Press.

Cronk, M. Sam, ed. 1990. *Sound of the Drum: Interviews with Native Musicians.* Brantford: Woodland Cultural Centre.

Deloria, Philip. 2004. *Indians in Unexpected Places.* Lawrence: University Press of Kansas.

Diamond Cavanagh, Beverley. 1992. "Christian Hymns in Eastern Woodlands Communities: Performance Contexts," in *Musical Repercussions of 1492: Explorations, Encounters, and Identities,* edited by Carol E. Robertson, 381–394. Washington: Smithsonian Institution.

Diamond, Beverley, et al. 1994. *Visions Of Sound.* Chicago: University of Chicago Press with Wilfrid Laurier University Press (Waterloo, ON).

Diamond, Beverley. 2002. "Native American Contemporary Music: The Women." In *Worlds of Music* (Berlin), special topics issue on Indigenous Popular Music in North America: Continuations and Innovations, 44/1: 9–35.

Dunbar-Hall, Peter, and Christopher Gibson. 2004. *Deadly Sounds, Deadly Places*: *Contemporary Aboriginal Music in Australia.* Sydney: University of New South Wales Press.

Ellingson, Ter. 2001. *The Myth of the Noble Savage.* Berkeley: University of California Press.

Ellis, Clyde, et al., eds. 2005. *Powwow.* Lincoln: University of Nebraska Press.

Feld, Steven. 1994. "From Schizophonia to Schizmogenesis: On the Discourses and the Commodification Practices of 'World Music' and 'World Beat.'" In *Music Grooves,* edited by Steven Feld and Charles Keil, 257–289. Chicago: University of Chicago Press.

Festinger, Leon. 1957. *A Theory of Cognitive Dissonance.* Stanford, CA: Stanford University Press.

Fewkes, Jesse Walter. 1890. "A Contribution to Passamaquoddy Folklore." *Journal of American Folklore* 3: 257–280.

Filewod, Alan. 2002. *Performing "Canada": The Nation Enacted in the Imagined Theatre.* Kamloops: Texual Studies in Canada 15.

Fogelson, Raymond, and Marcia Herndon. 1971. "The Cherokee Ballgame Cycle." *Ethnomusicology* 15/3: 327–352.

Folk on the Rocks. 2006. Canadian Broadcasting Corporation. CD. BC2-4161

Foster, Michael K. 1974. *From the Earth to Beyond the Sky: An Ethnographic Approach to Four Longhouse Iroquois Speech Events.* Ottawa: National Museums.

Ganahonyok. Grand River Polytechnic, Brantford, ON. N.d.

Gilman, Benjamin Ives. 1891. "Zuni Melodies." *Journal of American Ethnology and Archaeology* 1: 65–91.

Goertzen, Chris. 2001. "Powwows and Identity on the Piedmont and Coastal Plains of North Carolina." *Ethnomusicology* 45/1: 58–88.

Gordon, Tom. 2007. "Moravian Music in Labrador." *Newfoundland and Labrador Studies.* In press.

Green, Rayna. 1992. "Cherokee Stomp Dance." In *Native American Dance,* edited by Charlotte Heth, 177. Washington: Smithsonian Institution.

Green, Rayna. 1999. "Green Corn Ceremony." In *The British Museum Encyclopedia of Native North America,* edited by R. Green, 76. Bloomington: Indiana University Press.

Grenier, Line, and Val Morrison. 1994. "Policing French Language on Canadian Radio: The Twilight of the Popular Record Era." In *Rock and Popular Music: Politics, Policies and Institutions,* edited by T. Bennett, et al., 119–141, London: Routledge.

Grenier, Line, and Val Morrison. 1995."Quebec Sings 'E Uassuian': The Coming of Age of a Local Music Industry" in *Popular Music–Style and Identity*, edited by Will Straw et al., 127–136. Montreal: The Center for Research on Canada Cultural Industries.

Grey, Judith A. and Dorothy Sara Lee. 1988. *The Federal Cylinder Project: A Guide to Field Cylinder Collections in Federal Agencies*, Vol 2. Washington: Library of Congress.

Grinde, Donald A. Jr. "The Iroquois and the Development of American Government." *Historical Reflections* 21:2 (spring 1995), 301–318.

Hayden Taylor, Drew. 2004. "Rhythm Of Nations: Families meet up on the powwow trail under the spell of drum and dance." 54–59. *Canadian Geographic.* July/August 2004.

Hayden Taylor, Drew, comp. and ed. 2005. *Me Funny.* Vancouver: Douglas and McIntyre.

Heth, Charlotte, ed. 1992. *Native American Dance.* Washington: Museum of the American Indian.

Hewson, John and Beverley Diamond. 2007. "Santu's Song." *Newfoundland and Labrador Studies,* in press.

Hoefnagels, Anna 2001. "Powwows in Southwestern Ontario." PhD dissertation, York University, Toronto.

Howard, James. H. 1962. "The St. Anne's Day Celebration of the Micmac Indians, 1962." *Museum News* (South Dakota Museum) 26: 3–4 and 5–14.

Howard. James. H. 1983. "Pan-Indianism in Native American Music and Dance." *Ethnomusicology*. 27/1: 71–82.

Huenemann, Lynn F. 1992. "Northern Plains Dance." In *Native American Dance*, edited by Charlotte Heth, 125–148. Washington: Museum of the American Indian.

Hutchens, Jerry Lee. 2006. *Powwow Calendar 2006*. Summertown, TN: Native Voices.

Inuit Land Use and Occupancy Project. 1976. Ottawa: Department of Indian and Northern Affairs, Government of Canada.

Isaacs, Tony. www.indianhouse.com/frames.html.

Jackson, Jason Baird, and Victoria Lindsay Levine. 2000. " 'Thinking Music' and the Interactive Network in Woodland Intertribalism." Paper presented to the Society for Ethnomusicology, Toronto.

Jackson, Jason Baird, and Victoria Lindsay Levine. 2002. "Singing for Garfish: Music and Woodland Communities in Eastern Oklahoma." *Ethnomusicology* 46/2: 284–306.

Jones Bamman, Richard. 2001. "From 'I'm a Lapp,' to 'I'm a Saami': Popular Music and Changing Images of Indigenous Ethnicity in Scandinavia." *Journal of Intercultural Studies* 22/2: 189–210.

Kidwell, Clara Sue. 2002. "Native American Systems of Knowledge." In *A Companion to American Indian History*, edited by P. Deloria and N. Salisbury, 87–102. Oxford: Blackwell.

Kurath, Gertrude. 1968. *Dance and Song Rituals of Six Nations Reserve*. Ottawa: National Museums.

Lassiter, Luke. 1998. *The Power of Kiowa Song*. Tucson: University of Arizona Press.

Lawrence, Bonita. 2004. *"Real" Indians and Others: Mixed-Blood Urban Native Peoples and Indigenous Nationhood*. Lincoln: University of Nebraska Press.

Leacock, Eleanor. 1980. "Montagnais Women and the Jesuit Program for Colonization." In *Women and Colonization: Anthropological Perspectives*, edited by Mona Etienne and Eleanor Leacock, 25–42. New York: Praeger.

Lescarbot, Marc. [1606?] *The Theatre of Neptune*. Libretto reprint. Toronto: Champlain Society.

Levine, Victoria Lindsay. 1991. "Arzelie Langley and a Lost Pantribal Tradition." In *Ethnomusicology and Modern Music History,* edited by Stephen Blum, et al., 190–206. Urbana: University of Illinois Press.

Levine, Victoria Lindsay. 1993. "Musical Revitalization Among the Choctaw." *American Music* 11/4: 391–411.

Levine, Victoria Lindsay. 2002. *Writing American Indian Music: Historic Transcriptions, Notations, and Arrangements. Music of the United States of*

America, Volume 11. Middleton, Wisconsin: A-R Editions, Inc, editor-in-chief Richard Crawford, for the American Musicological Society.

Lipsitz, George. 1994. *Dangerous Crossroads: Popular Music, Postmodernism and the Poetics of Place.* London: Verso.

Martijn, Charles. 2003. "Early Mi'kmaq Presence in Southern Newfoundland: An Ethnohistorical Perspective, c. 1500–1763." *Newfoundland Labrador Studies* 19/1: 44–102.

McAllester, David. 1984. "North America/Native America." In *Worlds of Music,* edited by Jeff Todd Titon, et al., 12–63. New York: Schirmer Books.

McBride, Bunny. 2001. "Lucy Nicolar: The Artful Activism of a Penobscot Performer." In *Sifters: Native American Women's Lives,* edited by T. Perdue, 141–159. Oxford University Press.

Medicine, Beatrice. 2001. *Learning to Be an Anthropologist and Remaining 'Native.'* Urbana: University of Illinois Press.

Mihesuah, Devon A., ed. 1998. *Natives and Academics: Researching and Writing about American Indians.* Lincoln: University of Nebraska Press.

Mi'kmaq Book of Days. http://mrc.uccb.ns.ca/calendar.html.

Milliea, Mildred. 1989. "Micmac Catholicism in My Community. *Miigemeoei Alsotmagan Nemetgig.*" In *Papers of the Algonquian Conference* 20:262–266.

Mitchell, Tony. 1993. "World Music and the Popular Music Industry: An Australian View." *Ethnomusicology* 37/3: 309–338.

Nattiez, Jean-Jacques. 1983. "Some Aspects of Inuit Vocal Games." *Ethnomusicology* 27/3: 457–478.

Neuenfeldt. Karl. 1997. *The Didjeridu: From Arnhem Land to Internet.* Sydney: John Libbey.

Nunavut Arctic College. www.nac.nu.ca./publications/

Pisani, Michael. 2005. *Imagining Native America in Music.* New Haven: Yale University Press.

Powers, William K. 1990. *War Dance: Plains Indian Musical Performance.* Tucson: University of Arizona Press.

Prins, Harald E.L. 1989. "Two George Washington Medals: Missing Links in the Chain of Friendship Between the United States and the Wabanaki Confederacy." *Maine Historical Society Quarterly* 28/4: 226–234.

Prins, Harald E.L. 1996. *The Mi'kmaq: Resistance, Accommodation, and Cultural Survival.* Toronto: Harcourt Brace.

Richardson, Boyce. 1993. People of *Terra Nullius: betrayal and rebirth in aboriginal Canada.* Vancouver: Douglas and McIntyre.

Rollings, Willard Hughes. 2004. "Indians and Christianity." In *A Companion to American Indian History,* edited by Philip J. Deloria and Neal Salisbury, 121–138. Oxford: Blackwell.

Ross, Rupert. 1996/2006. *Returning to the Teachings: Exploring Aboriginal Justice.* Toronto: Penguin.

Sable, Trudy. 1998. "The Serpent Dance: The Multiple Layers of Meaning in a Mi'kmaw Dance." In *Papers of the 28th Algonquian Conference*, edited by David H. Pentland, 329–340. Ottawa: Carleton University.

Sable, Trudy. 2000. "Truth or Consequences? Creating a Dialogue between Science and Indigenous Knowledge Systems." Paper presented at ASA Conference 2000, School of Oriental and African Studies, London.

Scales, Christopher. 2004. "Powwow Music and the Aboriginal Recording Industry on the Northern Plains: Media, Technology, and Native American Music in the Late Twentieth Century." PhD dissertation, University of Illinois, Champaign-Urbana.

Shimony, Annemarie Anrod. 1994. *Conservatism Among the Iroquois at the Six Nations Reserve.* Syracuse: University of Syracuse Press.

Smith, Gordon. E. 1990. "Lee Cremo." In *The Sound of the Drum,* compiled by M.S. Cronk, 59–64. Brantford, ON: Woodland Cultural Centre.

Smith, Linda Tuhiwai. 1999. *Decolonizing Methodologies: Research and Indigenous Peoples.* London: Zed Books.

Smith, Nicholas. 1996. "The Wabanaki Trading Dance." In *Papers of the 27th Algonquian Conference,* edited by David H. Pentland, 238–247. Winnipeg: University of Winnipeg Press.

Smith, Nicholas. 2004. "Wabanaki Chief-Making and Cultural Change." In *Papers of the 35th Algonquian Conference,* edited by H.C. Wolfart, 389–405. Winnipeg: University of Winnipeg Press.

Speck, Frank G. 1922. *Beothuk and Micmac.* Indian Notes and Monographs. New York: Museum of the American Indian, Heye Foundation.

Speck, Frank G., and Leonard Broom. 1951. *Cherokee Dance and Drama.* Norman: University of Oklahoma Press.

Speck, Frank G. 1940/1997. *Penobscot Man.* Orono: University of Maine Press.

Spinney, Ann Morrison. 1999. "Dance Songs and Questions of Intercultural Influence in Wabanaki Ceremonial Life." In *Papers of the 30th Algonquian Conference,* edited by David H. Pentland, 334–350. Winnipeg: University of Winnipeg Press.

Spinney, Ann Morrison. 2006. "Medeolinuwok, Music, and Missionaries in Maine." In *Music in American Religious Experience,* edited by Philip V. Bohlman, et al., 57–82. New York: Oxford University Press.

Straw, Will, et al., eds. 1995. *Popular Music: Style and Identity.* Montreal: Research Centre for Canadian Cultural Industries and Institutions.

Stumpf, Carl. 1886. "Lieder der Bellakula-Indianer." *Vierteljahrsschrift für Musikwissenschaft* 2: 405–426.

Sweet, Jill. 2004. *Dances of the Tewa Indians: Expressions of New Life,* revised edition. Santa Fe: School of American Research Press.

Taborn, Karen. 2005. "Hybridity in Creek and Seminole Indian Christian Hymnody." Paper presented to the Society for Ethnomusicology, Atlanta, Georgia.

Thomas, Jake. *The Jake Thomas Learning Centre.* Online at www.tuscaroras.com./jtlc/The _Great_Law/great_law.html.

Tulk, Janice. 2006. "Cultural Revitalization and the Language of Tradition: Mi'kmaq Music in Miawpukek, Newfoundland." Paper presented to the Canadian Society for Traditional Music, Ottawa.

Vennum, Thomas. 1980. "A History of Objiwe Song Form." *Selected Reports in Ethnomusicology.* 3/2: 43–75. Los Angeles: University of California at Los Angeles.

Vennum, Thomas. 1982. *The Ojibwe Dance Drum: Its History and Construction.* Smithsonian Folklife Studies 2. Washington: Smithsonian Institution.

Vennum, Thomas, Jr. 1989. "Ojibway Music from Minnesota: Continuity and Change." St. Paul: Minnesota Historical Society.

Vizenor, Gerald. 1994/1999. *Manifest Manners: Narratives on Postindian Survivance.* Lincoln: University of Nebraska Press.

Von Rosen, Franziska. 1998. "Music, Visual Art, Stories: Conversations with a Community of Micmac Artists." PhD dissertation, Brown University.

Wallis, Wilson, and R.S. Wallis. 1955. *The Micmac Indians of Eastern Canada.* Minneapolis: University of Minnesota Press.

Warrior, Robert Allen. 1995. *Tribal Secrets: Recovering American Indian Intellectual Traditions.* Minneapolis: University of Minnesota Press.

Weisman, Brent Richards. 1999. *Unconquered People: Florida's Seminole and Miccosukee Indians.* Gainesville. University Press of Florida.

Wright-McLeod, Brian. 2005. *The Encyclopedia of Native Music: More Than a Century of Recordings from Wax Cylinder to the Internet.* Tucson: University of Arizona Press.

Resources

General

Brown, Jennifer, and Elizabeth Vibert, eds. 1996. *Reading Beyond Words: Contexts for Native History*. Peterborough: Broadview Press.

Browner, Tara. 1997. "'Breading the Indian Spirit': Thoughts on Musical Borrowing and the 'Indianist' Movement in American Music." *American Music* 15/3: 265–84.

Cronk, M.S., comp. 1990. *Sound of the Drum*. Brantford: Woodland Cultural Centre.

Deloria, Philip J., and Neal Salisbury, eds. 2004. *A Companion to American Indian History*. Oxford: Blackwell.

Dickason, Olive Patricia. 1992. *Canada's First Nations: A History of Founding Peoples from Earliest Times*. Toronto: McLelland and Stewart.

Dyck, Carrie. 2004. "Aboriginal Languages." In *Oxford Companion to Canadian History*, edited by Gerald Hallowell, 6–8. Don Mills, Ont.: Oxford Universty Press.

Ellingson, Ter. 2001. *The Myth of the Noble Savage*. Berkeley: University of California Press.

Grant, John Webster. 1984. *Moon of Wintertime: Missionaries and Indians of Canada in Encounter since 1534*. Toronto: University of Toronto Press.

Handbook of North American Indians. Vol. 5: *Arctic* (David Damas, ed. 1984); Vol. 6: *Subarctic* (June Helm, ed. 1981); Vol. 14: *Southeast* (Raymond D. Fogelson, ed. 2004); Vol. 15: *Northeast* (Bruce G. Trigger, ed. 1978). Washington: Smithsonian Institution.

Heth, Charlott, ed. 1992. *Native American Dance: Ceremonies and Social Traditions*. Washington: National Museum of the American Indian.

Jessup, Lynda, and Shannon Bagg. 2002. *On Aboriginal Representation in the Gallery*. Ottawa: Canadian Museum of Civilization.

Keeling, Richard. 1989. *Women in North American Indian Music*. Ann Arbor: Society for Ethnomusicology.

Keeling, Richard. 1997. *North American Indian Music: A Guide to Published Sources and Selected Recordings*. New York: Garland Publishing.

Levine, Victoria Lindsay 1998. "American Indian Musics, Past and Present." In *Cambridge History of American Music,* edited by David Nicholls, 3–29. Cambridge: Cambridge University Press.

McMaster, Gerald, and Lee-Ann Martin, eds. 1992. *Indigena: Contemporary Native Perspectives.* Ottawa: Canadian Museum of Civilization.

Miller, J.R. 1991. *Sweet Promises: A Reader on Indian-White Relations in Canada.* Toronto: University of Toronto Press.

Native American Expressive Culture. 1994. Ithaca: Akwe:kon Press and the National Museum of the American Indian.

Pisani, Michael V. 2005. *Imagining Native America in Music.* New Haven: Yale University Press.

Smith, Claire, and Graeme Ward, eds. 2000. *Indigenous Cultures in an Interconnected World.* St. Leonards, NSW: Allen and Unwin.

Smith, Linda Tuhiwai. 1999. *Decolonizing Methodologies: Research and Indigenous Peoples.* London: Zed Books.

Trigger, Bruce, and Wilcomb E. Washburn, eds. 1996. *The Cambridge History of the Native Peoples of the Americas.* Cambridge: Cambridge University Press.

Wright-McLeod, Brian. 2005. *The Encyclopedia of Native Music.* Tucson: University of Arizona Press.

CD Compilations

The websites of Canyon Records, Indian House, Sound of America Records, Sunshine Records, and Arbor Records are good places to find audio recordings. Websites below also list information for individual artists.

Among the large number of compilation CDs produced, the following are good starting points for teachers and students:

Smithsonian Folkways.

___1973. *Anthology of North American Indian and Eskimo Music.* FW04541.

___1994. *Creation's Journey.* SFW40410.

___1995. *Heartbeat. Voices of First Nations Women.* SFW40415.

___1997. *Wood that Sings.* SFW40472.

___1998. *Heartbeat 2. More Voices of First Nations Women.* SFW40455.

___2004. *The Beautiful Beyond. Christian Hyms in Native Languages.* SFW40480.

Wright-McLeod, Brian, comp. *The Soundtrack of a People: A Companion to The Encyclopedia of Native Music.* EMI Music Canada. 09463 11696 2 5, 2005.

Websites

www.goodminds.com. A First Nations publications center with good online catalogue, particularly for print materials. Music is not a specific focus.

www.fourdirectionsteachings.com. Resources provided by specific First Nations.

www.hanksville.org. Go to "Index of Native American Music Resources on the Internet."

www.nativedance.ca. A media-rich site constructed in collaboration with several universities and First Nations cultural centers in Canada. The project was coordinated by Dr. Elaine Keillor of Carleton University.

www.nativedrums.ca. A media-rich site constructed in collaboration with several universities and First Nations cultural centers in Canada. The project was coordinated by Dr. Elaine Keillor of Carleton University.

www.nativeradio.com. Claims to be the largest site for the distribution of broadcasts of Native American music.

www.nativeculture.com/lisamitten/music/. For more than two decades, Lisa Mitten has provided a huge service by maintaining a current bibliography and discography for Native American music scholars.

TIK

Augustine, Stephen. 1997. "Mi'kmaq Knowledge in the Mi'kmaq Creation Story: Lasting Words and Lasting Deeds." Online at http://faculty.uccb.ca/mhunter/mi'kmaqcreation.htm.

Battiste, M. 1998. Enabling the Autumn Seed: Toward a Decolonized Approach toward Aboriginal Knowledge, Language and Education. *Canadian Journal of Native Education*, 22(1): 16–27.

Battiste, Marie. 2000. *Reclaiming Indigenous Voice and Vision.* Vancouver: University of British Columbia Press.

Battiste, Marie. 2000. "What is Indigenous Knowledge?" In *Protecting Indigenous Knowledge and Heritage,* edited by Marie Battiste and James (Sa' ke'j) Youngblood Henderson, 35–58, Saskatoon: Purich.

Brant Castellano, Marlene. 2000. "Updating Aboriginal Traditions of Knowledge." In *Indigenous Knowledges in Global Contexts — Multiple Readings of Our World*, edited by G. J. Sefa Dei, et al., 21–36. Toronto: University of Toronto Press.

Brown, Michael F. 2003. *Who Owns Native Culture?* Cambridge: Harvard University Press.

Dei, George J. Sefa, et al. 2000. *Indigenous Knowledges in Global Contexts.* Toronto: University of Toronto Press.

Grim, John. 2001. *Indigenous Traditions and Ecology.* Cambridge, MA: Harvard Center for the Study of World Religions.

Hennepe, Sheila Te. 1997. "Respectful Research: That Is What My People Say, You Learn it From the Story." In. *Radical In<ter>ventions: Identity, Politics, and Difference in Educational Praxis,* edited by Suzanne de Castell and Mary Bryson, 153–182. Albany: State University of New York Press.

Kidwell, Clara Sue. 2002. "Native American Systems of Knowledge." In *A Companion to Amerian Indian History,* edited by P. Deloria and N. Salisbury, 87–102. Oxford: Blackwell.

King, Thomas. 2003. *The Truth About Stories*. Toronto: Anansi.

Macedo, Donaldo. 1999. "Decolonizing Indigenous Knowledge." In *What is Indigenous Knowledge: Voices from the Academy,* edited by Ladislaus M. Semali, et al. 1–2. New York: Falmer Press.

McConaghy, Cathryn. 2000. *Rethinking Indigenous Education: Culturalism, Colonialism and the Politics of Knowing*. Flaxton: Post Pressed.

Newhouse, David. 2004. "Indigenous Knowledge in a Multicultural World." *Native Studies Review* 15/2: 139–54.

Posey, Darrell. 2004. *Indigenous Knowledge and Ethics*. New York: Routledge.

Von Lewinski, S. 2004. *Indigenous Heritage and Intellectual Property : Genetic Resources, Traditional Knowledge and Folklore*. New York: Kluwer Law International.

Websites

www.unesco.org/most/bpindi.htm. Best Practices on Indigenous Knowledge. A database maintained by UNESCO.

www.native-languages.org. Excellent links to language sites but also to sites that provide reliable information about each nation's history, cultural institutions, and contemporary artists.

Inuit

Arna'naaq, Luke, et al. 1987. "Drumbeats of the Past: Qilaujjarnirijait Kinguvaattinnut." In *Isumasi—Your Thoughts*. 1/1: 9–19. Rankin Inlet: Inuit Cultural Institute.

Conlon, Paula Thistle. 1992. Drum-Dance Songs of the Iglulik Inuit in the Northern Baffin Island Area: A Study of their Structures. PhD dissertation, University of Montreal.

Hauser, Michael. 1978. "Inuit Songs from Southwest Baffin Island in Cross-Cultural Context." *Etudes/Inuit/Studies* 1: 55–83 and 2: 71–105.

Hauser, Michael. 1992. *Greenlandic Eskimo Music*. Copenhagen: Sisimiut.

Lutz, Maija. 1978. *The Effects of Acculturation on Eskimo Music of Cumberland Peninsula*. Ottawa: National Museums of Canada.

Lutz, Maija. 1982. *Musical Traditions of the Labrador Coast Inuit*. Ottawa: National Museums of Canada.

Nattiez, Jean Jacques. 1982, "Comparisons Within a Culture: The Example of The *Katajjaq* of the Inuit." *Cross-Cultural Perspectives on Music*, edited by In Robert Falck and Timothy Rice, Toronto: University of Toronto Press. 134–140.

Nattiez, Jean-Jacques. 1999 "Inuit Throat Games and Siberian Throat Singing: A Comparative, Historical, and Semiological Approach." *Ethnomusicology* 43/3: 399–418.

Peacock, F. W. 1977. "Music of Nain Inuit." *Inuttituut*. Winter: 52–58.

Pelinski, Ramon, et al., eds. 1979. *Inuit Songs from Eskimo Point*. Ottawa: Musée national de l'Homme.

Pelinski, Ramon. 1981. *La Musique des Inuit du Caribou. Cinq perspectives methodologiques*. Montreal: Les Presses de L'Université de Montréal.

Saladin d'Anglure, B. 1978. "Entre cri et chant: les katajjait, un genre musical feminine." *Inuit Studies*, vol. 2: 85–94.

Vascotto, Norma. 2001. "A Musical Family: Drum Song Transmission and Oral History in an Inuit Family of Musicians in the Central Arctic." PhD dissertation, University of Toronto.

Audio Recordings

Canada. Jeux Vocaux des Inuit. HM 52. Ocora, 1990.

Chants et jeux traditionnels inuits. Inuit Traditional Songs and Games. Radio Canada SQN108. Boots Records, 1984. (Documentation by Nicole Beaudry).

The Eskimos of Hudson Bay and Alaska. Folkways FW4444, 1955.

Inuit Games and Songs. Philips 6586036, 1978.

The Inuit (Eskimos) of the Arctic Circle. Recorded in 1980. Vols. 1–2. Lyrichord LLst 7379 and 7380, n.d.

Inuit Throat and Harp Songs (Eskimo Women's Music of Povungnituk) / Chants Inuit - gorge et guimbarde (Musique des esquimaudes de Povungnituk): Canadian Music Heritage MH-001 1981.

Songs of the Iglulik Inuit. Berlin. Berlin Museum Collection CD 19, 1993.

Musiques et Chants Inuits. Eskimo Point et Rankin Inlet. Compiled by Ramon Pelinski. UMM C-202, 1990.

Rankin Inlet Music Festival 1998–99. 2-CD set.

Truly Something. True North Concerts. Yellowknife: CBC North, 2000.

Other Media

Atanarjuaq. Film directed by Zacharie Kunuk and produced by Isuma Productions, Iglook, Nunavut. 2001.

Websites

www.virtualmuseum.ca. Tuhaalruuqtut Ancestral Sounds. 100 audio-visual examples of historical photographs, narrative, and traditional music by Baker Lake elders, 1998, 2000, from the Inuit Heritage Centre in Baker Lake. A 2-CD set with some of the same material is available under the title *Tuhaalruuqtut*. Volumes 1 and 2, produced by Sally Qimmiu'naaq Webster. (Baker Lake: Inuit Heritage Centre).

Atlantic First Nations

Clifford, James. 1988. "Identity in Mashpee." In *The Predicament of Culture: Twentieth Century Ethnography*. Berkeley: University of California Press, 277–348.

Densmore, Frances. 1956. *Seminole Music*. United States Government Printing Office.

Diamond, Beverley. 1992."Christian Hymns in Eastern Woodlands Communities: Performance Contexts." In *Musical Repercussions of 1492: Explorations, Encounters, and Identities,* edited by Carol E. Robertson, 381–394. Washington: Smithsonian Institution.

Feintuch, Burt, and David H. Watters. 2005. *The Encyclopedia of New England*. London: Yale University Press.

Foster, Michael K., and William Cowan, eds. 1998. *In Search of New England's Native Past: Selected Essays by Gordon M. Day*. Amherst: University of Massachusetts Press.

Mailhot, Jose. 1997. *The People of Sheshatshit*. Translated by Axel Harvey. St. John's, NL: ISER Books.

Marshall, Ingeborg. 2001. *The Beothuk*. St. John's: Newfoundland Historical Society.

McCoy, George, as told to H.F. Fulling. 1961. *The True Meaning of Stomp Dance, History of the Stomp Dance of the Sacred Fire of the Cherokee Indian Nations*. Blackgum: Marshall Walker.

Parsons, Elsie Clews. 1925. "Micmac Folklore." *Journal of American Folklore*. 38: 55–133.

Paul, Margaret. 1999. "'Every Song You Sing Just Keeps Getting Better and Better. '" *In the Words of Elders: Aboriginal Cultures in Transition,* edited by Peter Kulchyski, et al., 3–36. Toronto: University of Toronto Press.

Rand, Silas T. 1894. *Legends of the Micmacs*. New York: Longmans, Green and Co.

Smith, Gordon E. 1994. "Lee Cremo: Narratives About a Micmac Fiddler." In *Canadian Music: Issues of Hegemony and Identity*, edited by Beverley Diamond and Robert Witmer, 541–556. Toronto: Canadian Scholars Press.

Spinney, Ann Morrison. 2005. "Passamaquoddy Social and Ceremonial Songs." In *Algonquian Spirit*, edited by Brian Swann, 84–98. Lincoln: University of Nebraska Press.

Tanner, Adrian. 1979. *Bringing Home Animals: Religious Ideology and Mode of Production of the Mistassini Cree Hunters*. St. John's, NL: ISER Books.

Von Rosen, Franziska. 1998. "Music, Visual Art, Stories: Conversations With a Community of Micmac Artists." PhD dissertation, Brown University.

Wallis, W.D., and Wallis. R.S. 1955. *The Micmac Indians of Eastern Canada.* Minneapolis: The University of Minnesota.

Whitehead, Ruth Holmes. 1988. *Stories from the Six Worlds: Micmac Legends*. Halifax: Nimbus Publishing.

Audio Recordings

Free Spirit. MicMac (Mi'Kmaq) Songs. Winnipeg: Sunshine Records SSCT 4093, n.d.

Miawpukek. Conne River. Se't A'newey Mi'kmaq Choir and Spu'ji'j Drummers. Amber Music, 2000.

Mi'kmaq Chants. Denny family. Kewniq Recordings Productions/Spectrum Records RC505, n.d.

Music of the Algonkians. Folkways FW04253, 1972.

Micmac Traditional Songs. George Paul. Independent cassette, ca. 1980.

Puamuna. Montagnais Hunting Songs. Radio Canada SQN-100, Boots Records, 1982.

Songs of the Seminole Indians of Florida. Folkways FW04383, 1972.

Sons of Membertou. *Wapna'kik. The People of the Dawn.* Sydney: Atlantica Music ATL0001, n.d.

Spirit of the Dawn. *Songs of the Wabanaki.* Old Town, ME: Penobscot Indian Arts, 2001.

Stomp Dance. (Muscogee, Seminole.) Vols. 1–4. Indian House IH 3003–06, recorded 1991, n.d.

Traditional Music of Maine. Orono, ME: Northeast Archives of Folklore and Oral History, 1988.

Where the Ravens Rest: Cherokee Traditional Songs of Walker Calhoun. Cullowhee, NC: Mountain Heritage Center Recording, 1991.

Wolastoqiyik lintuwakonawa: Maliseet songs / chants malécites. CD: 12 songs. Province of New Brunswick with the Canadian Museum of Civilization CA2 NB CULSPO W54, 2004.

Video/DVD

From the Heart. Three Maritime Folk Musicians. (One is Sarah Denny, Mi'kmaq elder.) Sydney: University College of Cape Breton.

Kwa'nu'te. Mi'kmaq and Maliseet Artists. Produced by Catherine Martin (Mi'kmaq). Ottawa: National Film Board of Canada.

Websites

http://mrc.uccb.ns.ca. Mi'kmaq Resource Centre, University College of Cape Breton (now Cape Breton University).

Haudenosaunee

Alfred, Taiaiake. 1999. *Peace, Power, Righteousness: An Indigenous Manifesto.* New York: Oxford University Press.

Conklin, Harold, and William C. Sturtevant. 1953. "Seneca Indian Singing Tools at Coldspring Longhouse: Musical Instruments of the Modern Iroquois." *Proceedings of the American Philosophical Society.* 97:262–290.

Cornelius, Richard, and Terence J. O'Grady. 1987. "Reclaiming a Tradition: The Soaring Eagles of Oneida." *Ethnomusicology* 31/2: 261–272.

Foster, Michael, et al. eds. 1984. *Extending the Rafters: Interdisciplinary Approaches to Iroquoian Studies.* Albany: State University of New York Press.

Heth, Charlotte. 1979. "Stylistic Similarities in Cherokee and Iroquois Music." *Journal of Cherokee Studies* 4/3: 128–162.

Hill, Richard. W. S. 1996. "Patterns of Expression: Beadwork in the Life of the Iroquois." In *Gifts of the Spirit.* Exhibition catalogue. Peabody Essex Museum.

Key, Amos Jr. 2005. "The Successes of Immersion/Bilingual Education at Six Nations of the Grand River." *Wadrihwa* (Woodland Cultural Centre, Brantford, ON) 15–20.

Krouse, Susan Applegate. 2001. "Traditional Iroquois Socials: Maintaining Identity in the City." *American Indian Quarterly* 25/ 3: 400–408.

Kurath, Gertrude. 1964. "Iroquois Music and Dance: Ceremonial Arts of Two Seneca Longhouses." *Bureau of American Ethnology Bulletin* 187: 1–259.

LaFrance, Ron. 1992. "Inside the Longhouse: Dances of the Haudenosaunce." In *Native American Dance,* edited by Charlotte Heth, 19–32. Washington: National Museum of the American Indian.

The Great Peace. CD-ROM. GoodMinds Distribution (Six Nations).

Weaver, Sally. 1972. *Medicine and Politics Among the Grand River Iroquois: A Study of the Non-Conservatives.* Ottawa: National Museums.

CDs and DVDs

Allegany Singers. *Earth Songs.* Volumes 1–4. Self-produced, 2002.

Ganohgwatroho:no Henadrenoto:ta (Sour Springs Longhouse Male Singers). Earth Songs. Volume 1 self–produced, n.d.

Iroquois Social Dance Songs. Three volumes, 33 1/3 rpm. Ohsweken, ON: Iroqrafts, 1969.

Iroquois Social Music. Music Gallery 001, 1974.

Seneca Social Dance Music. Folkways FW04072, 1980.

We Will All Sing/ Edwadrenodo:nyo. Six Nations Women Singers. SOAR 175, 1996.

Songs and Dances of the Eastern Indians from Medicine Spring and Allegany. New World Records NW 337, 1975.

Songs and Dances of the Great Lakes Indians. Folkways FW04003, 1956.

Websites

www.ohwejagehka.com. Information about many genres of social dance music.

Powwow and Contemporary Music

Browner, Tara. 2000. "Making and Singing Pow-wow Songs: Text, Form and the Significance of Culture-Based Analysis." *Ethnomusicology* 44(2): 214–233.

Burton, Bryan. 1993. *Moving Within the Circle: Contemporary Native American Music and Dance*. Danbury, CT: World Music Press.

Cornelius, Richard, and Terence O'Grady. 1987. "Reclaiming a Tradition: The Soaring Eagles of Oneida." *Ethnomusicology* 31/2: 261–272.

Corrigan, Samuel W. 1970. "The Plains Indian Powwow: Cultural Integration in Manitoba and Saskatchewan." *Anthropologica* 12: 253–277.

Diamond, Beverley. 2002. "Native American Contemporary Music: The Women." *The World of Music* 44/1: 11–40.

Diamond, Beverley. 2005. "Media as Social Action: Native American Musicians in the Recording Studio." In Wired *for Sound: Engineering and Technology in Sonic Cultures,* edited by Paul Greene and Thomas Porcello, 118–137. Hanover: Wesleyan University Press.

Ellis, Clyde. 2003. *A Dancing People: Powwow Culture on the Southern Plains.* Lawrence: University Press of Kansas.

Fletcher, Alice C. 1893/1994. *A Study of Omaha Indian Music*. Lincoln: University of Nebraska Press.

Goertzen, Chris. 2001. "Powwows and Identity on the Piedmont and Coastal Plains of North Carolina." *Ethnomusicology* 45/1: 558–588.

Gorbman, Claudia. 2000. "Scoring the Indian: Music in the Liberal Western." In *Western Music and Its Others,* edited by Georgina Born and David Hesmondhalgh, 234–253. Los Angeles: University of California Press.

Hatton, Orin T. 1986. "In the Tradition: Grass Dance Musical Style and Female Powwow Singers." *Ethnomusicology* 30/2: 197–221.

Hoefnagels, Anna. 2002. "Powwow Songs: Traveling Songs and Changing Protocol." *The World of Music* 44/1: 227–236.

Keillor, Elaine.1995. "The Emergence of Postcolonial Musical Expressions of Aboriginal Peoples within Canada." *Cultural Studies* 9/1: 106–124.

Mattern, Mark. 1996. "The Powwow as a Public Arena for Negotiating Unity and Diversity in American Indian Life." *American Indian Culture and Research Journal* 20/4: 183–201.

Neuenfeldt, Karl. 2002. "http://www.nativeamericanmusic.com : Marketing Recordings in an Interconnected World," The *World of Music* 44/1: 93–102.

Powers, William K. 1987. "Regulating a War Dance: Nonverbal Cues Around an Oglala Drum." In *Beyond the Vision*, 37–49, Norman: University of Oklahoma Press.

Powers, William K. 1990. *War Dance: Plains Indian Musical Performance*. Tucson and London: The University of Arizona Press:

Samuels, David. *Putting a Song on Top of It: Expression and Identity on the San Carlos Apache Reservation*. Tucson: Arizona University Press.

Scales, Christopher. 2002. "The Politics and Aesthetics of Recording: A Comparative Canadian Case Study of Powwow and Contemporary Native American Music." *The World of Music* 44/1: 41–60.

Scales, Christopher. 2004. "Powwow Music and the Aboriginal Recording industry on the Northern Plains: Media, Technology, and Native American Music in the Late Twentieth Century." PhD dissertation, University of Illinois, Urbana.

Vennum, Thomas Jr. 1980. "A History of Ojibwa Song Form." *Selected Reports in Ethnomusicology* 3/2: 42–75.

Wright McLeod, Brian. 1996. "Bury My Heart: A Brief History of Resistance and Protest in Contemporary Native Music." *Aboriginal Voices* 5/2: 36–39, 49.

Young Bear, Severt, and R.D. Theisz. 1994. *Standing in the Light: A Lakota Way of Seeing*. Lincoln: University of Nebraska Press.

CD/DVD

*Powwow Tr*ail. Episode 1: The Drum; Episode 2: The Songs. (9-part series in production.) Winnipeg: Arbor Records, 2004 -

CDs of powwow groups are widely available. See online catalogues of Canyon Records, Arbor Records, Sunshine Records, and others listed in Wright-McLeod (2005).

Given the large output of CDs of contemporary Native American music, a selective listing here would be arbitrary. Readers should consult Wright-McLeod (2005) or websites listed below to find specific artists or genres.

Websites

www.powwow.com. Podcasts from live events; extensive information about current activity and historical studies.

www.canab.com. For information about the Canadian Aboriginal Music Awards and biographies of nominated artists.

www.nativeamericanmusicawards.com. For information about the Nammys.

www.gatheringofnations.com. Internet radio with both powwow and contemporary popular music.

www.nativeculture.com/lisamitten/music.html. Maintained by Lisa Mitten.

Some Key Publications on the Music and Dance of Other First Nations

Asch, Michael. 1988. *Kinship and the Drum Dance in a Northern Dene Community*. N.p.: Boreal Institute for Northern Studies.

Black Bear, Ben Sr., and R.D. Theisz. 1976. *Songs and Dances of the Lakota*. Aberdeen, SD: Northern Plains Press.

Fletcher, Alice C., and Francis La Flesche. 1893. *A Study of Omaha Indian Music*. (reprinted 1994; Lincoln: University of Nebraska Press.)

Frisbie, Charlotte Johnson. 1967/1993. *Kinaaldá: A Study of the Navaho Girl's Puberty Ceremony*. Salt Lake City: University of Utah Press.

Goodman, Linda, and Helma Swan. 2003. *Singing the Songs of My Ancestors: The Life and Music of Helma Swan, Makah Elder*. Norman: University of Oklahoma Press.

Haefer, J. Richard. 1977. *Papago Music and Dance*. Navajo Community College Press. Tsaile: Arizona.

Howard, James H., and Victoria Lindsay Levine. 1990. *Choctaw Music and Dance*. Norman: University of Oklahoma Press.

Jackson, Jason Baird. 2003. *Yuchi Ceremonial Life*. Lincoln: University of Nebraska Press.

Levine, Victoria Lindsay. 1993. "Musical Revitalization Among the Choctaw." *American Music*. 11/4: 391–411.

McAllester. David. 1949. *Peyote Music*. New York: Viking Fund Publications in Anthropology.

Merriam, Alan P. 1967. *Ethnomusicology of the Flathead Indians*. Chicago: Aldine.

Nettl, Bruno. 1989. *Blackfoot Musical Thought: Comparative Perspectives*. Kent: Kent State University Press.

Powers, William K. 1980. "Oglala Song Terminology." *Selected Reports in Ethnomusicology* 3/2: 23–41.

Ridington, Robin, and Jillian Ridington. 2006. *When You Sing it Now, Just Like New: First Nations Poetics, Voices, and Representations*. Lincoln: University of Nebraska Press.

Smyth, Willie, and Esmé Ryan, eds. 1999. *Spirit of the First People: Native American Music Traditions*. Seattle: University of Washington Press.

Sweet, Jill Drayson. 2004. *Dances of Tewa Indians: Expressions of New Life*. Revised edition. Santa Fe: School of American Research Press.

Vander, Judith. 1988. *Songprints: The Musical Experience of Five Shoshone Women*. Urbana: University of Illinois Press. (An article-length study focusing on the same women was published in Keeling, 1989.)

Vennum, Thomas. 1982. *The Ojibwe Dance Drum: Its History and Construction*. Smithsonian Folklife Studies no. 2. Washington: Smithsonian Institution. Published in conjunction with a 42-minute film (*The Drummaker*) shot in Wisconsin.

Vennum, Thomas. 1989. *Ojibway Music from Minnesota: A Century of Song for Voice and Drum*, St. Paul: Minnesota Historical Society Press.

Index